The Taste
of an Olive

The Taste of an Olive

A Southside of Chicago Memoir

Patrick J. Finn

DEDICATION

To Mary Finn

My Wife, My Editor, My Best Friend Forever

CONTENTS

PART I: THE WAY WE WERE

PART II: THE TASTE AN OF OLIVE

ACKNOWLEDGEMENTS

Book design by Amy Finn
Moral support by Molly Finn
Editorial support by Mary Finn

Author's Note

I've written this book to tell the story of my life as it was through my High School years that ended in 1953. A good deal of what I want to share is about racism and ethnic strife. To tell the story I've chosen to use the actual slurs that were used at the time recognizing that these words can be hard to read.

Part I.

THE WAY WE WERE

Chapter 1.

PRELUDE

A checkered career. I have had what some might call a checkered career. I was born in Chicago in 1935. I am the eighth of nine children — six boys and three girls. All my brothers followed my father's trade, plumbing. I am the only one of my siblings to attend college. Not being one for half-measures, I eventually earned a Ph.D. I'm from an Irish Catholic family, and I am the only one of my siblings to leave the fold. Again, no half measures, I eventually became a Quaker. I have lived in Chicago; Alaska; two cities in Scotland — Edinburgh and Glasgow; Highland Park, New Jersey; Williamsville, New York; Buffalo, New York; and Los Angeles, California (for several years in Chinatown).

I graduated from Chicago Teachers College in 1959. In the following years I taught eighth grade at Fiske Elementary School, an all-Black public school on Chicago's Southside and at an On-Base School at Fort Greeley Army Base in Alaska. I taught tenth grade high school English in a newly opened, purportedly progressive high school in Norridge, Illinois — a working-class suburb just outside Chicago. At that time, I had quite traditional views on educating working-class students and I found many of the attempted progressive reforms

1

unfeasible and I repeatedly said so. At the end of the year my contract was not renewed. That is to say, I was fired. Fair enough.

I edited middle school literature anthologies at Scott Foresman (now Pearson Education). I earned a Ph.D. at the University of Chicago, and I spent the last year of my doctoral studies as a 'Visiting Scholar' at Edinburgh University in Scotland. Later I spent a sabbatical year in Scotland while my wife, Mary Finn, was a visiting scholar at Glasgow University. My first teaching job after I received my Ph.D. was a one-year appointment at Rutgers University filling in for a professor who was on sabbatical. I spent my final thirty years of teaching at the Graduate School of Education at The State University of New York at Buffalo where I taught students preparing to be reading and language arts grade school teachers.

I have published a half dozen articles in scholarly journals and two college textbooks — one on teaching reading and one on teaching writing. These were not run-away best sellers, but in 2000, the year I retired from teaching, I published *Literacy with an Attitude: Educating Working-Class Children in their own Self-Interest*, a book I had been working on for the previous ten years. It became one of the ten best-sellers in its publisher's (State University of New York Press) history. I published a second edition of that book in 2009.

For ten years after I retired, I kept busy with speaking and consulting engagements; I co-edited a book with my wife,

2

and I published a few more articles — one of which, "Unrest in Grosvenor Square: Preparing for Power in Elite Boarding Schools and Working-Class Public Schools," earned an award from The Center for Working Class Studies at Georgetown University.

But then a couple of years ago I simply had nothing more to say on the topics I had been writing and speaking on for forty years. And so I thought I'd write a memoir, at least for my children and grandchildren, but who was I kidding? For the past fifty years I hardly write a paragraph that I don't think to myself, "I think I could turn this into something I could publish somewhere."

I no sooner got started than a question began to loom ever and ever larger. Why didn't my mother like me? It's not as though this thought had never occurred to me previously; but it became obvious to me that I could not ignore this question and continue to tell my story. This, as I have learned since, is not an unusual experience for the memoirist, and the answer is frequently, "It was your own damned fault." And yes, it was my own damned fault.

Chapter 2.

MOTHER'S DEATH

I travel to be with her. In her 84th year, my mother went into the hospital for a somewhat routine surgery, and the surgeon found her organs were riddled with cancer that had gone undetected. They stitched her up and told her the surgery was a success but that she would have a long recovery. This was 1985 when doctors frequently lied to cancer patients about the diagnosis that was thought to be too difficult for the patient to bear.

I drove to Chicago from my home in Buffalo, New York to visit her while she was still in the hospital. I brought with me my first book entitled *Helping Children Learn to Read*. It had just been delivered to me from the publisher. The dedication page read:

to my mother
Alverna Smerz Finn

My mother was born to Czech (what everyone in Chicago at the time called "Bohemian") parents, Albert and Josepha Smerz. But because she was "Mrs. Finn" in an Irish

Catholic neighborhood and had nine children, she gave up bothering to tell people that she was not Irish. In fact, no one called her Alverna. Everyone called her "Mrs. Finn" or just "Finn." Having the book in my hand provided a reason for my visit—other than that I had driven ten hours from Buffalo to visit her after what everyone was pretending was a successful routine surgery.

I don't remember her being very excited about my book, published by Random House, no less. I attributed her lack of enthusiasm to the fact that she was, after all, recovering from surgery. My sister Mary told me later that using mother's Bohemian maiden name—was "inspired." The fact that my mother bragged about my book to others but never actually complimented me was typical of our relationship. I think she might have had the same relationship with all of my brothers and sisters.

During the hospital visit my mother said, "I'm just glad it's not the big 'C.'" It took me a moment to understand that she meant, "I'm glad they didn't find cancer." I tried to agree nonchalantly, "Yes. You dodged that bullet!" I wondered if I had been very convincing. After several days in the hospital my mother went to stay with my sister Mary, believing that when she was well enough, she would return to her own place where she lived with my brother Jack.

After a couple of weeks, and against her doctor's advice, some of my brothers and sisters gathered in her bedroom to tell her that indeed she did have cancer and that she was not expected to live more than a few more weeks. She was pretty unhappy about the deception, but in a little while she understood what motivated it and suggested they send out for Popeye's chicken! My mother was very smart, and I think she probably knew all long what the game was.

I visited her again for a weekend after she knew she was dying. She was mostly sedated at this point but she did wake up and talk for short periods of time. She said that she had had a good life and implied (but did not actually say) that she was ready to die. As I sat by her bed, I wondered if there was something that I would wish at some time in the future I had said to her, but I could think of nothing.

I took her hand when I thought she was sleeping and after a while she awoke and withdrew her hand gently and said, "I like holding your hand, Paddy. It's just uncomfortable." I think of that from time to time when remembering her, and when I'm feeling a little morose, which is not all that unusual for me, how that sums up so much of our relationship.

My final visit came a few weeks later. I had lived in Buffalo since 1973. The semester was coming to an end and I decided that when classes ended, I would go to Chicago and stay until she died. The day after my last class I was scheduled to do a presentation to a group of Buffalo school principals at 8:00 in the morning. I did that presentation, left for Chicago around 10:00 a.m. and got to my sister's house around 7:00

pm. When I entered her bedroom my mother was conscious and said, "Hello, Paddy." I believe those were her last words.

For the remainder of the evening my sister Mary, my brother Jack, two of Mary's daughters and I sat at the kitchen table just outside the bedroom where my mother lay in a coma. We drank tea, discussed preparations for her funeral, listened to her breathing, and listened for her to stop breathing.

The nurse supplied by hospice arrived around midnight, and thinking my mother would live till morning, Jack and Mary's daughters went home, and I went to bed in the basement dormitory where Mary's five boys slept when they were children. Only Mary remained awake. About 4 a.m. she called me from the top of the basement stairs to say the nurse believed my mother was dying. Despite the need to hurry, I had to stop in the bathroom before going upstairs. It was the many cups of tea that we drank the night before. By the time I got to the top of the stairs my mother had been gone for a few minutes. She had never regained consciousness.

At my mother's wake, Aunt Bess, my mother's sister, asked me if I had my book with me. My mother had told her about it and about the dedication. It did not surprise me at all that my mother had told my sister and my aunt that she was delighted that I had dedicated the book to her, and that I had referred to her as Alverna *Smerz* Finn, but she had not actually said that to me. I don't remember even feeling sad. There was a distance between us that I had become quite accustomed to.

7

My wife once told me that she thought there was a strange formality in the way my mother and I spoke to one another. She was right.

Chapter 3.

AN UNLIKELY COUPLE

My parents were a decidedly unlikely couple when they were married on the Southside of Chicago in 1920. He was very handsome. He stood about five-foot-eight, had black curly hair, and blue eyes. My mother was very pretty, but she stood around five-foot two and she was overweight. Very overweight. There is a short Carl Sandberg poem that goes like this:

> *This here phizzog*
> *Somebody handed it to you - am I right?*
> *Somebody said, "Here's yours, now go see what*
> *you can do with it."*
> *It was like a package marked: "No goods*
> *exchanged after being taken away."*

The phizzog someone handed my mother was no bargain, but she dispelled forthwith any idea that anyone might have had that she was intimidated by them or by the occasion. She was unapologetic. She was self-assured. She was admirable. She came on like gangbusters. In a situation that seemed to call for a little formality or decorum, she was likely to say something just a little crude—saying in effect, "Let's cut the crap." In fact, on many occasions, she said

9

precisely, "Let's cut the crap." She was smart, fun-loving, proud, assertive, gutsy, intelligent, ambitious, interested, interesting, and combative. People loved her.

My father was born in 1898. He came from a dirt-poor Irish family. His father died in the Alcoholics Ward at Cook County Hospital, and his mother supported her six children by scrubbing floors in downtown Chicago office buildings. My mother, on the other hand, came from a large, fairly prosperous Czechoslovakian or Bohemian family. Her father was a building contractor.

But it was not just the economic status of their families that made their marriage unusual. At that time the Southside of Chicago was a collection of ethnic neighborhoods, all of them Catholic, but always on the brink of war with one another. And so, in the parlance of that time and place, she was a "Bohunk" and he was a "Mick." Marriages between these two warring camps were rare. In fact, Catholic clergy sometimes referred to them as "Mixed Marriages."

My parents met in Chicago on the eve of the "Roaring Twenties." My mother had gone to work at the Illinois Bell Telephone Company when she left eighth grade at age 14, and so she would have been in the workforce for four years. She had arranged to go out with friends to the White City Ballroom which was a remnant of the 1893 Columbian Exposition that celebrated the four-hundredth anniversary of Columbus's 1492 "discovery" of America. The Exposition started a year late due to building difficulties.

My mother had no doubt stashed her outfit and makeup at a friend's house and put them on after she left her parents' house. This was the era of "the flapper." Her father was very patriarchal, and he objected to girls reading the newspaper because it was unseemly for women to be interested in politics. He sure as hell would have objected to rouge and powder and lipstick, let alone going to White City Ballroom with other single girls.

My father had just returned to Chicago from service in the Navy and he was probably wearing his Navy blues. She must have captivated him with her willingness to step out, take charge, and charm the socks off of everyone in the room. They were married soon thereafter. My mother never talked about their wedding. No wedding anniversary was ever mentioned. The one thing my mother told me about her wedding was that she and my father were married by Father Bobal who was pastor of St. Procopius, the Czech Catholic Church near 18th and Racine Street in Chicago.

My parents were both interested in and active in local politics. He was involved in the rough and tumble days of creating the Chicago Plumbers Union Local 130 in the 1920's and 1930s, and he remained a close associate of Steve Bailey, President of Local 130. He knew the famous Richard M. Daley who was to become the mayor of Chicago in 1955. They were raised in the same neighborhood. My father was also involved in numerous fraternal organizations such as Veterans of Foreign Wars, the Holy Name Society, and the Loyal Order of Hibernians.

From my earliest days I remember that my mother canvassed our precinct for the Democratic Party during election campaigns and worked at the polls on election days. She sold poppies on busy Chicago street-corners for the Veterans of Foreign Wars on Memorial Day (now Veterans Day). She was also active in St. Leo Parish organizations such as the Altar and Rosary Society, and she also met fairly frequently with women friends. Several of her friends had a coffee klatch which they called "The Dirty Six A.C." The "A.C." stood for "After Cooking."

The differences between my parents' families were not just ethnic rivalry. The Smerzes epitomized the traits of Bohemians in Chicago in the 1920s — Catholic, but moderately so; fairly prosperous; financially savvy; and somewhat circumspect. The Finns epitomized the traits of the Irish in Chicago in the 1920s — very Catholic; very poor; not financially savvy; and very boisterous.

Albert Smerz and Josepha Kalal, my mother's parents, were born in Prague in about 1850. They were part of a large number of Bohemian (Czech) immigrants who settled on Chicago's Southside between 1850 and 1900 when Chicago had the third-largest Czech population of any city in the world after Prague and Vienna. Albert's parents were prosperous enough to send him to America to avoid being drafted into the Austro-Hungarian army. I know nothing of Josepha's story except that she and Albert were not acquainted in Bohemia. They met and married in Chicago in about 1870. Albert became a fairly prosperous building contractor, and his sons became tradesmen and contractors also.

The Smerzes were Catholic, but I do not think they took their religion very seriously. Nineteenth century Czech nationalists were "free thinkers" and socialists who identified Catholicism as an Austro-Hungarian import that had been forced upon them. And while many Czech immigrants in the United States remained Catholic, the influence of the church on their lives was pale compared to the influence of the church on the Irish. In Chicago, Bohemians became known for their Savings and Loan Institutions, and I learned to my surprise that that might have been the result of socialist influence. I knew nothing of this when I was growing up because my mother rarely spoke about her family.

She did tell me that her father did not permit the girls in the family to read the newspaper, and so she would take it from the garbage pail in the kitchen and read it in the attic. That was like her. She had always been interested in politics and she always had a mind of her own. She told several of my siblings and their children that she wished she could have become a United States Senator, and that she would have been good at it.

The Smerzes had seven children. My mother was their fifth child. She was named "Albena" after an older brother named Albert who died in infancy. After she was born, her parents had two more children, a girl named Elizabeth (Bess) and a son also named Albert. When my mother finished grade school, she changed her name to Alverna. Her brothers and sisters always called her "Alby."

I don't think Josepha ever spoke English fluently and all my mother's siblings were bilingual — English and Bohemian. They all married people descended from eastern Europeans. My mother's oldest sister and her husband (Marie and Joseph Koredik) owned a ma and pa grocery store near 22nd and Ashland in a neighborhood known as "Pilsen." It was named after the city in Bohemia where Pilsen beer originated.

Bohemian was spoken more often than English in Aunt Marie and Uncle Joe's store. My mother and her brothers and sisters used a few Bohemian words or phrases when they were together — always accompanied by laughter — but she never spoke Bohemian in our home. Once while I was in high-school I asked her to try speaking Bohemian at dinner so that I might pick up a little. She was not interested.

The Smerzes owned their own home and, judging from a family photograph taken around 1910, they were fairly well off. The photograph was taken in a professional photography studio. The father and all the boys wore well-fitted suits with white shirts with stiff collars and ties — the kind of collars that were starched and ironed as stiff as cardboard and buttoned on to shirts that were laundered separately. The mother and girls wore expensive looking dresses with hemlines nearly at their ankles. My mother was only eight or ten and unlike any of her siblings she was overweight.

My mother's mother had died before I was born and her father not long after. One of my earliest memories is of visiting a very old man with my mother. I think that was her father, but it might have been my Uncle Joe Koredik. Uncle Joe's right leg was amputated below the knee, and he had some difficulty getting around. Because of that I thought he was much older than he really was. I never knew how he lost his leg.

I knew my aunts and uncles — Marie, Bess, Jose, Albert, and Joe. There was also an Aunt Ann whom I rarely saw. My mother really disliked her. From my mother's rare references to Ann, I got the impression that she disapproved of my mother's hell-raising when she was single and the fact that she married an Irishman.

My father's father, James Finn, was born in Ireland. There are two stories about his precise place of birth. We always believed that he came from Cork, but I was told by a librarian in the Irish National Library Archives in Dublin that many American Irish believe their ancestors came from Cork because the boat for America left from Cork. On my father's death certificate his father's place of birth is listed as Dublin, Ireland. That information was supplied by my brother Jim, who was about 20 at the time, and I have no idea where he got it. I'm thinking he was thinking, "Dublin is close enough — what's your next question?" That would have been Jim.

My father's mother was Nora Shea. One of my nieces has traced Nora's family to Castlegregory, Ireland, a tiny village near Tralee. Her family emigrated from Ireland to Nova Scotia, Canada at least two generations before she was born. At some point, the family moved to Maine. The oldest girl of that generation married a Protestant and was disowned. She and her husband moved to Chicago where he became a successful painting contractor.

One by one her brothers and sisters moved to Chicago where her husband set them up with jobs. They remained Catholic. My grandmother, Nora Shea, was the child of one of the children of this generation. She met James Finn in Chicago and they married. My father was their sixth child born in 1898.

My father's family lived just west of the Chicago Stock Yards—in back of the yards—which was considered a badge of honor among the Chicago Irish. There is a song that was sung at Finn family parties that expresses it well: "In Back of the Yards".

In back of the yards
In back of the yards
In old Chicago Town.
Where each fellow and gal
Is a regular pal.
They'll never let you down.
Where an ace is an ace
Any time any place.
You're sure to win their kindest regards.

16

So I feel mighty proud, And I'm shouting out loud
That I hale from in back of the yards!

My grandfather, James Finn, was a "hide inspector" (I can only guess what that means) in Chicago's stockyards. He died when Nora was carrying their seventh child. The story my mother told was that James was walking home from work and suffered an epileptic seizure while cutting through a vacant lot, what we called a "prairie" in Chicago. Tall grass (actually prairie grass) grew in vacant lots and there were often paths through them that pedestrians used for short cuts. Someone found him unconscious and called the police. The police thought he was drunk and threw him into a cell at the local precinct. They found him dead the next morning.

There is an alternate story: James died in the alcohol ward at the Cook County Hospital. That version came from my father's cousin whom my oldest sister, Norrine, talked to around 1980. I think the latter version is closer to the truth. Nora lived another 10 years or so after my grandfather died. She got the children to bed, locked the house, and took streetcars the six miles downtown to scrub floors in office buildings. She came home, got the children off to school or work (the oldest three were girls who would have left school at around age 13 or 14). She then slept through the morning and afternoon. There was no such thing as help from the county in those days.

None of my father's sisters lived much past forty. They all died long before I was born. There is a story that one of them died of a broken heart. Norrine learned through

17

cemetery records that there is an infant buried in the grave of one of my grandparents in Holy Sepulcher Cemetery in Chicago. That might be part of the "broken heart" story.

The only story that I ever heard of my father's boyhood was of his older brothers Jim and Ed. In those days a number of excursion boats took people from Chicago across the lake to Michigan City, Indiana for a day at an amusement park. On a Saturday in July of 1915, one of these boats — *The Eastland*-- capsized while still at the dock and 844 people died. The event became known as "The Eastland Disaster".

My Uncle Ed was supposed to have been on that boat, but somehow, he had not yet boarded when the disaster struck. My Uncle Jim, the older brother, heard of the unfolding disaster over the radio and took a streetcar down to the Clark Street Bridge. He joined the crowd of onlookers and soon spied Ed among them. He was so overcome with emotion that he ran up to Ed, spun him around and punched him in the nose with all his might.

There is an alternate story. A local Southside Chicago newspaper published a story saying that one James Finn had heard that his brother Edward Finn was on *The Eastland* and rushed down to the dock where he saved six drowning men. I am sure the latter story would have become the family lore if it had been true, and so I tend to go with the "punch in the nose version."

My father had three brothers: Jim, Ed, and George. Jim was in the army during World War I, and he was confined to a wheelchair for as long as I knew him. The story was that he had arthritis. He was married to my Aunt Alice who was several years older and who was a very sour individual. Family lore has it that Jim had married Alice to take care of his younger brothers when his mother died, and his infirmity was not arthritis; it was the result of syphilis that he had contracted in Europe during World War I that had gone untreated. Syphilis might have accounted for the fact that Jim and Alice never had children. Untreated, syphilis often leaves men sterile.

Ed was an electrician. He was married to Aunt Sis. She always reminded me of Maggie, a character in "Bringing Up Father," a comic strip that was on the front page of the comics section of the *Sunday Chicago Tribune* when I was a little boy. Maggie is the wife of Jiggs, an Irish bricklayer who wins the lottery and comes into a lot of money. Maggie and Jigs have a daughter, Nora, who is quite sweet and beautiful.

Maggie takes on the affectations that she believes are appropriate for a woman in high society, with comic effect. It was Aunt Sis's makeup and the affected way she spoke that reminded me of Maggie. Aunt Sis would take what she imagined an elegant pose and say something like, "They ain't got nothing there that would be of any interest to me!" — "there" being a place where she had not been given the deference she believed she deserved.

I was too young to get the joke about Maggie's putting on airs. I must have picked that up from my mother. I did know Aunt Sis was a phony. Like Maggie and Jiggs, Ed and Sis had one daughter, Delores. She was, in fact, very beautiful and actually did seem quite refined. She married a divorced man which was spoken of in hushed tones in our Irish Catholic family.

My father was the third boy. He had one younger brother, George. George married Aunt Mary and they had three daughters: Mary Jane, Patsy, and Georgine. George had pure white hair by the time he was 30 and was movie-star handsome. He was a Chicago policeman, and for a while he was bodyguard to the president of Colgate-Palmolive Company—apparently, because in a well-tailored suit, he was highly presentable among the country club set. Aunt Mary was a telephone operator at the Illinois Bell Telephone Company from the time she was a teenager, and she went back to work after each of the girls was born.

George came down with acute arthritis when he was about 40 that badly crippled him. He was in Hines Veterans Hospital in Maywood, a suburb of Chicago, for months afterwards. My father used to take a car full of us out on Sunday afternoons to "visit Uncle George." The children could not go in to visit, so we waited in the car and my father would take us for ice cream afterwards. This gave my mother a well-deserved afternoon off.

Aunt Mary and the three girls lived with us for several months while George was in Hines Hospital. That added four more people to the eleven of us! They slept in the cavernous unfinished attic. Aunt Mary helped with dinner when she could, depending on the shift she was working. She would help with the dishes afterwards and then announce, "I'm going to walk up to the corner to buy a paper." Actually, she walked up to The Three Pats, one of the four or five bars on Halsted Street, to sit at the bar and have a few beers. But she always did come home with the *Chicago Tribune.*

When George got out of the hospital his career as a policeman was over. He became a bookie, an illegal off-track horse-racing betting operation. His "office" was the corner barstool at The Three Pats. He may have shared the proceeds with the officer on the beat, or he was given a pass because he was an ex-policeman. That's the way it was.

George and Ed and their wives were great partiers. Groups of them and friends used to go to Cedar Lake, Indiana, probably a three-hour drive from Chicago given the cars and roads at that time. There were said to have been two to three day, twenty-four hours-a-day poker games on these outings. People left the game, slept or ate, and returned to the game that never stopped going. No one ever went near the water.

I don't think my father or mother were ever part of these Cedar Lake excursions, but my father and his brothers were known to entertain at house parties. They actually created routines that they performed together. My father once recited a poem "The Face on the Bar Room Floor" at a party in our kitchen (probably a graduation, or Confirmation party). The poem is some 80 lines long and starts:

> *'Twas a balmy summer's evening*
> *and a goodly crowd was there*
> *Which well-nigh filled Joe's barroom*
> *on the corner of the square,*
> *And as songs and witty stories came*
> *through the open door*
> *A vagabond crept slowly in and*
> *posed upon the floor.*

The vagabond reveals that he was once an artist, and he has come to ruin as a result of his unrequited love for a beautiful woman. The closing stanza reads:

> *Another drink, and with chalk in*
> *hand, the vagabond began,*
> *To sketch a face that well might buy*
> *the soul of any man.*
> *Then, as he placed another lock*
> *upon that shapely head,*
> *With a fearful shriek, he leaped and*
> *fell across the picture — dead!*

This was a dramatic recitation, from memory, and included pantomiming the narrator entering the bar, telling his doleful story and drawing the beautiful face of the woman he loved and that left him, to the dramatic last stanza where

22

he dies of a broken heart and falls on the face on the bar room floor.

My mother seemed to enjoy these parties when they were at our house. They were not all that frequent, perhaps once or twice a year for some occasion, like a Confirmation or First Communion party for one of us children, but she never went to these Finn bashes elsewhere. I think she felt she had nothing in common with Sis who thought herself the last word in elegance and Mary, a party girl.

I think this was one of the reasons that my mother did not seem to like my father. She put in hard weeks of work raising nine children and running a huge house, and she was left alone on Saturday night—and many weeknights as well when my father went out to meetings of the many organizations he belonged to.

All of this partying went on between 1918, when my father and his brothers returned from World War I, and 1945—the end of World War II. My father died in 1948 at age 50, and his three brothers, Jim, Ed, and George, all died in the next few years. Not one of them lived much past 50. I think the chronic illnesses and early demise of the entire family were the result of their poor nutrition as young children.

A few years after my father's death my mother went to work at NuPhone, a telephone answering service above Walgreens at 79th and Halsted. My mother worked the night shift—midnight to 8:00 a.m.—and George's wife, Aunt Mary, called her frequently in the middle of the night to cry about what a hellish existence she led during those years of partying with a playboy husband and that my mother had taken the better part, staying home and taking care of her family that was a model of an Irish Catholic family that made good. The irony was that my mother was not Irish and it was her influence—the Bohemian influence—that was largely the reason for the financial success of our family.

Chapter 4.

WONDERFUL FAMILY

I am the eighth of my parents' nine children — Norrine, Dan, Jim, Mary, Jack and Joan (twins), Bob, me, and Mickey — three girls, six boys. We were born roughly two years apart, starting with Norrine in 1922 and lastly with Mickey in 1940. I was born in 1935. Since there were so many of us at the dinner table, older siblings were assigned to take care of one of the younger children.

Norrine was thirteen years older than I, and I became "Norrine's boy." In many ways I thought of myself as Norrine's boy for the remainder of her life. She died in 2015 when she was 91 and I was 79.

When Norrine was only three, she contracted polio which left her left leg severely paralyzed. She walked with a heavy brace until she was about twelve. At twelve, she announced she would no longer wear the brace. The doctor told my parents it wouldn't hurt if she tried, but she would simply never walk without it. She never wore a brace again until she was over 80 when at last, indeed, she could not walk without it.

Basil Bernstein, a British sociologist, observed that girls who are born first in large, working-class families often have a gentrifying effect on their much younger siblings, especially younger brothers. Older girls in charge of younger brothers are typically not allowed to use corporal punishment or even threats of corporal punishment to keep their young charges in line. As a result, an older sister is more likely to negotiate with the younger brother regarding his behavior, and the boy has something more like a typical middle-class upbringing than a boy who is raised exclusively by a working-class mother. This has an effect not only on the boy's behavior, but also on his use of language.

I loved being with Norrine and talking to her. Once when I was about ten, she was getting ready to go out, and I was telling her about a movie I had seen, and I followed her into the very small first-floor bathroom. I pushed past her so I could get along-side the sink where she was putting on make-up. I continued talking the entire time. She pointed out that she *was* in the bathroom and maybe I'd be willing to step outside and let her finish what she was doing! We laughed, of course, but that is how it was between Norrine and me.

The first "theme" I wrote in college English 101 was about Norrine, her grit, and how she influenced my life — my being the eighth of nine children in a working-class family. My theme earned an "A," and that convinced me that I could do this college stuff.

When my oldest brother Dan was born, Norrine was just two and she called him "Brud" — attempting to say "brother." The name stuck and everyone in the family called him Brud for the rest of his life. **Jim,** the third child, was born just a year after Brud. Brud and Jim were remarkably handsome and what we called "tough" in our Irish-Catholic, working-class, Southside Chicago neighborhood. They were in their middle teens when World War II started and they both joined the Navy — probably lying about their ages with my parents' connivance.

They got out of the Navy after the war and became plumbers (my father's trade). They were both married by the time they were 21 and went on to have large families (Brud, nine children and Jim, seven). By the time they were 30, Brud was foreman of the plumbing shop for the entire City of Chicago and Jim was a business agent for the powerful Chicago Plumbers Union. Their youthful rise to powerful positions was accounted for in part by the fact that my father had connections in union circles and in Mayor Daley's administration. They had what was called in Chicago, "clout."

Brud and Jim both died of heart attacks before their 45th birthdays. I believe they died so young because they drove themselves so hard. They not only had large families that they provided for lavishly, but they were the go-to guys when any of us needed a job, or a traffic ticket fixed, or when we were in more serious trouble. Brud and Jim were my mother's golden boys.

I was never part of their world. Once when I was in college but living at home, Brud called me at about 10 p.m. and asked me to join him and Jim at a nearby tavern. We drank until about 3 a.m. — closing time for some bars in Chicago. I went home and slept-in, missing my morning classes. They went home, slept a few hours, showered, and were on deck at very demanding jobs by 7:30 a.m. the next morning. I think that routine was fairly common. I seem to have flunked my audition because I was never again invited to join them at a tavern, but I think these Finn-brother events occurred pretty regularly.

My sisters Mary and Joan were several years older than I, and I have few memories of them from before I was in high school by which time, they had both married World War II veterans and proceeded to have large families — Mary, ten children, and Joan, eleven.

Jack, Joan's twin, was born with a heart condition and he was never entirely well his whole life. He probably never stood more than 5'-5" and he had a foot deformity that caused him to limp slightly. He went to Gompers School for Crippled Children. We were unsparing in our classifications in those days. These were not "special needs children;" they were not "differently-abled children." They were cripples.

After Gompers, Jack went to Calumet, the public high school for our neighborhood. He graduated after four years, and through Brud and Jim's influence he landed jobs in the Chicago Parks Department and the Water Department. He eventually became a journeyman plumber and installed water meters for the city.

When he was about 27, Jack checked in to the Cook County Tuberculosis Sanitarium for several months. He never had tuberculosis, but he was chronically tired and needed rest, and so the TB sanitarium was deemed the place for him. While there, doctors decided that Jack was a suitable candidate for a recently developed surgery that would fix the kind of heart problem he was born with.

The surgery was still considered experimental at the time. They packed the patient in an ice blanket and cooled his body down until the heart beat very slowly and the surgery was done between beats. I was quite certain at the time that Jack thought he was going to die during the operation, but he was just so tired all the time that he was ready to face death.

A few days before the surgery Jack had his hair cut very short — all but shaved. My mother was furious. I thought at the time that she was worried about what people would say if he died. He would be waked in an open coffin, as was the custom in those days, and his shaved head would have made an awful appearance. He survived the operation and lived another 35 years in better health but never tip-top.

When Jack actually did die, his hair once again became an issue. He was waked in an open coffin, and when the family first arrived at the funeral parlor for the "private viewing," we were all startled to find that the undertaker had put a lot of dressing on Jack's hair and slicked it straight back off his forehead. Jack's hair was curly and he always wore it a little shaggy with a kind of studied messiness. No one would have recognized Jack with the slicked back hair and Irene, Jack's partner of many years, said, "We should mess it up!" My niece Mary Ann did just that and it looked like Jack and we all have another fond, bittersweet memory of him.

Jack never married. He lived with my mother (more accurately, my mother lived with him) and he took care of her after everyone else left home. Jack had what we called a long engagement with Irene Muzzy whom he met when he and my mother moved into the first-floor apartment in her two-flat. Jack was 35 then, and where he slept most nights was a question one did not ask.

Jack made a journeyman plumber's salary and had no dependents and he led a pretty frugal existence. Before I left home, I shared a bedroom with him and there was a stack of US government bonds in the top drawer of our dresser several inches thick that he purchased with payroll withholdings. He was very generous and pretty regularly helped others out with loans, many of which were never repaid. He had two extravagances: he always drove a Pontiac four-door sedan and he flew first-class on airplanes.

I think Jack and Irene never married because they were both Catholic and Irene was divorced. At my mother's funeral nearly everyone in the church including me — who had not set foot in a Catholic church for 20 years — went to the alter rail to receive Communion—everyone except for Jack and Irene. They were "practicing Catholics" but "living in sin." It made me very sad. I went to Communion although, according to church rules as a "fallen-away" Catholic, I was not supposed to receive Communion. I thought at the time it would please my mother, but she more likely would have seen it as one more example of my not fitting-in and persistently reminding everyone of that fact.

Irene moved in with Jack when my mother died and they lived together for the remainder of Jack's life—another 15 years. He died of a heart attack at age 69 getting out of his Pontiac in an icy parking lot of a supermarket. A man saw him fall and thought he had slipped on the ice. He was dead when the man got to him.

Jack gets my nomination for the bravest of all the Finns. He was dealt a really bad hand and led a life worthy of admiration. He had a Catholic funeral, and if anyone ever deserved heaven it was Jack. I don't know if Irene received Communion at Jack's funeral mass. I did, and one of my nieces was acting as a "Eucharistic Minister" (she distributed Communion), and I watched her turn pale as she saw me approach the altar rail.

My brother Bob was born after the twins. My mother had "a nervous breakdown" immediately after his birth. Today they would undoubtedly call it post-partum depression, and if anyone ever had reasons for being depressed, it was her. Bob was the seventh child and Norrine, the oldest child, was just eleven. My mother had two babies (Jack and Joan, the twins) in diapers at home. This was during the Great Depression and my father was out of work. We were no doubt "on relief" which would have been a source of deep humiliation for her. I never heard her once refer to the fact that we had ever been on relief.

I was 21 when I first learned about my mother's breakdown. I had gone to a family party at Jim and his wife Helen's house, and I had brought a date, Theresa Walsh. It was pretty much a standard Finn family party. Twenty or so of us — brothers, sisters, spouses, and friends — arrived around eight dressed to the nines. We had a few drinks, and around 10 there would be a buffet of ham, potato salad, coleslaw, and sandwich rolls, and more drinks.

By midnight, everyone would have gravitated to the kitchen, and we began to sing old favorites like "In Back of the Yards," "Heart of my Heart," and "Just a Little Street" (where old friends meet). There would be a song and a lot of banter when someone would start a new song and we would all join in. In addition, many of us had our own solo number. After a song and a little banter someone would say, for example, "Let's hear from Helen (Jim's wife.)" Another would say, "Yah, Helen, 'You Made Me Love You (Helen's song),'" and after a little more coaxing Helen would sing "You Made Me Love You."

This was followed by raucous cheering, shouting, applause, and more banter. And so the night went 'til people started to leave at 2 or 3 a. m. There would have been a number of drivers "under the influence" on the streets of the Southside of Chicago for the next half-hour. As far as I know, no one ever got stopped, and if stopped, they talked their way out of a ticket. This was Chicago and we were Irish. We had never heard the phrase "White privilege," but we all knew how it worked.

In the midst of this particular party, my brother Jim said to my mother, "Yah, Ma, remember that time you went nuts?" I didn't know what he meant, and I didn't pay particular attention to it at the time, but the next day I heard my mother on the telephone, angry and crying and talking to Jim and saying. "Why would you say that in front of that girl?" It turned out that "that girl" was Theresa Walsh, my date—an outsider. That of course prompted me to ask my older sisters what this was all about.

What I learned was this: After Bob's birth my mother was showing signs of acute depression. My mother was taken home after four or five days (the normal time a woman would have stayed in the hospital after giving birth in those days), but Bob, the newborn, was sent to stay with my father's cousin whom we called Aunt Mame, and the county supplied a housekeeper for our home for several months. Norrine said that the housekeeper was a German immigrant with a storm trooper mentality who would not let my mother into her (the housekeeper's) kitchen. Norrine found the part about the housekeeper and the kitchen very amusing.

My mother deeply resented anyone telling her how to raise her children. If she had an enemies list, most educated, childless women would have been on it and social workers would rank near the top. Teaching nuns were a somewhat different matter. The nuns at St. Leo Grammar School, which we all attended, probably had only a two-year teaching degree, and my mother once told me that they mostly came from farms and small towns. In other words, they did not have any intellectual pretentions, and they did not engage in psychology which she would undoubtedly have referred to as "that crap."

Unlike any of the rest of us, Bob flagrantly disobeyed my mother. She was not above administering the "back of the hand" if one of her boys (never the girls) was misbehaving within her reach, but only once did she ever administer a beating. Bob was the recipient. Jack, Bob, and I were about 12, 10, and 8 at the time. We had been rolling a tennis ball from between parked cars onto the streetcar tracks on Halsted Street—a street with very heavy traffic and a streetcar line.

The object was to get the ball to land on the track (which was recessed into the brick pavement) so the streetcar would roll over it and crush it. When the ball did not land on the track (which it never did) one of us would run from between parked cars onto the busy street to retrieve it. It was sort of a game. A neighbor had seen us and told my mother. The three of us were summoned into the kitchen, and so the three of us were present, but only Bob got the licking. He was no doubt unrepentant. That's how it was between Bob and my mother.

We were a very loving family, and where there are nine children at different stages of growing up, there were shifting "alliances" that developed over a span of years. Bob was just two years older than I, and from the time I was around six to ten I absolutely adored him. When I was about six, my sister Norrine, who was out of high school and working by then, took my sisters Mary and Joan, and my brothers Jack and Bob and me downtown to have our pictures taken at a photography studio as a Christmas present for my parents. I distinctly remember that the studio was run by a family of little people or as we said then "midgets." (Years later I mentioned this, about the little people, to Norrine and she said she did not remember that and she thinks she would have!)

Anyway, downtown Chicago is and was a very busy place and Norrine was shepherding five of us, four of whom were under 10 on crowded busy streets. I thought Bob was wandering away from us and I began shouting for him to come back. Heads turned among our fellow pedestrians and Norrine was mortified that I had attracted so much attention. I might have been fairly screaming. Norrine grabbed hold of my shoulder and told me to behave myself. I thought that was unjustified, given the fact that Bobby might have gotten lost, but I soon got over it. The trip ended successfully, and those pictures are around somewhere to this day.

But the trip downtown is just part of this memory about Bob. On nearly every Sunday afternoon Bob, Jack, and I and sometimes others walked the three or four blocks from our house to the Cosmo Movie Theater on Halsted Street—14 cents admission for a double feature. We did not go to see a particular movie. We went every Sunday no matter what was playing. Sometimes the movies were pretty scary. I remember particularly "The Thirteenth Guest," a 1932 movie starring a very young Ginger Rogers.

At that time Bob, Jack, and I (ages 8, 10 and 6) shared a double bed—me in the middle because I was youngest. We were very vigilant to see that the others did not encroach on our one-third of the mattress, but when I would get scared at night, usually remembering a movie, I would tell Bob I was afraid and ask if I could touch his foot. He'd say ok and I'd move my foot over just a little to barely touch his foot and I'd feel safe. Sometimes, being there and feeling safe, I would remember the downtown incident and think, "I don't care if I did get yelled at. He would have gotten lost and I'm glad I yelled."

Like Brud and Jim, Bob left school early. He joined the Marines at age 17 and served in Korea. When he was discharged, he became a plumber like my older brothers, and married Kay Gibson, a classmate of mine at St. Leo Grammar School, who was one of the most beautiful girls I have ever known. They had seven children. Bob died at age 40—a combination of the family heart history and some hard living.

I weighed over 9 pounds at birth and it was a very difficult delivery (which my mother mentioned to me once or twice, not maliciously, but as a matter of fact). I sustained an injury to my left shoulder in the process that left my left arm slightly paralyzed and a little shorter and weaker than the right arm. The problem is not so much in the strength of the arm, as it is in the arm's limited mobility. I cannot raise it more than shoulder height. I learned from a college swim instructor that this condition has a name — Erb's Palsy.

I always thought it was the result of an injured muscle, but it's the result of damage to a nerve center in the shoulder that results in paralysis in the arm. It is often the result of "gestational diabetes," high sugar in a pregnant woman's blood. This sometimes results in extraordinary weight gain in the mother, high birth weight babies, difficult births, and birth-injuries to the baby. My mother was seriously overweight her whole life. I don't know if she gained additional weight while carrying me.

I discovered when I looked into Erb's Palsy at age 80 that one symptom is a victim's eyelid on the affected side droops slightly. Mine does. I once asked a girl I dated in college if she had ever noticed this and she said, yes, she had. She said she never mentioned it because it would be "like giving a knife to a child." The point being that some people found it a little sexy.

As I grew-up I could not catch, and I hated sports. I did play a little sandlot baseball and football (as little as possible), but I was always last to be chosen for the team. On one occasion a boy yelled to the batter, "Hit to left field. He can't catch." Yes, that was me in left field. One day Bob tried to teach me to catch because he knew how important it was for a boy to play baseball.

I don't remember how cooperative I was, but he soon gave up. At around the same time Brud tried to teach me to catch but he, too, soon gave up. He was wearing his Navy uniform at the time, so it must have been during World War II. I would have been around 8 or 9. Truth to tell, I might have learned to catch if I had tried. I just didn't care. I don't think I would have liked sports even if I had had shoulders like Charles Atlas.

When I was very young my mother would supervise me as I exercised the arm, using my fingers to crawl up the wall and stretch the muscles in my arm and shoulder, and she would massage my shoulder with some sort of oil. She meant business, and it hurt. These sessions did not produce any progress and they lasted only a short time. I've seen nothing in looking into Erb's Palsy to indicate that exercises would have helped.

Mickey (yes, Mickey Finn), the sixth boy and ninth child, was born when I was five. As the baby of the family, he had a special place in my mother's heart. I don't think he ever had the golden-boy status of Brud and Jim, but he was surely a favorite.

Mickey was not a boy who ever went willingly to school, but I don't think he was ever in danger of not passing, and he did not give the sisters at St. Leo any trouble. He went from St. Leo Grammar School to St. Leo High School. At the end of first year, he transferred to Calumet. The following year my mother was called to Calumet because Mickey was repeatedly sleeping in class.

This was not such a terrible infraction, certainly not grounds for suspension or expulsion, but rather than go herself, my mother sent Kay, Bob's newly married wife, to the school to sort things out. Kay was only about 20 years old at the time and did not have a lot of what one might call respect for authority.

I have a vivid picture in my mind of what might have transpired: Kay enters the counselor's office wearing a short skirt and white cowboy boots --"Go-Go Boots" they were called at the time. Playing in Kay's head are lines from a popular song:

> *These boots are made for walking.*
> *And that's just what they'll do.*
> *One of these days these boots*
> *Are gonna walk all over you!*

I wasn't there, of course, and I don't know what happened, but I feel certain that that image accurately captures the essence of the scene. Kay did, in fact, have a pair of such boots, but that song was not written for another ten years.

The upshot of this episode was that Mickey was expelled from Calumet and sent to "continuation school" — a school that met one or two days a week for students who were excluded from school but too young to leave in terms of Illinois compulsory school attendance laws. He did not actually attend continuation school for very long. Brud arranged it so that he was marked present at the school every day until he was old enough to leave school legally — Finn family clout at work again.

Meanwhile, Brud and Jim set him up as an apprentice glazer. He was putting glass windows in Chicago skyscrapers in all weather at age 16. That sometimes meant zero and below weather. He joined the Navy at 17, served 18 months on Guam, was discharged, married his high school sweetheart, had four children, and was a journeyman plumber all by the time he was 27. Being nearly five years older than Mickey, I had little in common with him when we were kids, but after we were both married, he became and remains my closet sibling.

Chapter 5.

7736 SOUTH UNION AVENUE

I was born in 1935, not the Best of Times. It was the mid-point of the Great Depression. Three years earlier forty-three thousand World War I veterans and their families had marched on Washington D.C. to demand the bonus promised them eight years earlier. President Hoover sent troops and armored tanks and evicted the marchers. Franklin Delano Roosevelt was elected president later that year and the veterans' bonus was paid in 1936.

My father had served in the Navy during World War I and with his bonus, probably just around $300, my parents put a down payment on a house at 7736 South Union Avenue on the Southside of Chicago. They paid around $2,500. I have no doubt that my mother with her Bohemian economic savvy had a lot to say about how the bonus was spent. My father's three brothers had all served in the armed forces during World War I. They undoubtedly received the same bonus. None of them ever owned a home.

The house on Union Avenue gave our family security and a certain status in our largely Irish Catholic Parish—St. Leo. It was a huge seven-room frame house built a generation earlier for the gentry. There was a small front lawn and a large back yard with a garage that opened onto an alley. The front porch was big enough for a two-seat swing suspended from the ceiling and several pieces of outdoor furniture.

The front door opened onto a hall with a beautiful walnut staircase up to the second floor. There were four rooms on the first floor, the usual front room (which we always referred to as "the parlor"), dining room, and kitchen, but there was also a "music room" tucked in behind the dining room and next to the kitchen. Off the hall between the kitchen and dining room there was a "butler's pantry"—a small room with floor-to-ceiling cabinets with drawers at the bottom for table linens and silver ware and shelves behind glass doors at the top for dishes and glass ware. A bit further down the hall was a door to the dining room designed for serving the meal—presumably by a maid. There were wood burning fireplaces in both the parlor and dining room.

There was a very plain back stairway to the second floor behind a door off the kitchen (for servants, again). Another door off the kitchen opened to the space under the staircase forming a small closet. There was a door connecting the music room and kitchen as well. In the very large kitchen, there was a large old-fashioned porcelain sink with a single drain board that stood on legs. The water pipes and drainpipe were in plain view.

There were no cabinets or counters in the kitchen, but there was ample room for a gas stove, a refrigerator, a kitchen table, and six chairs. This big kitchen was the setting for the graduation and Confirmation parties. My father's "The Face on the Barroom Floor" rendition was here at one of those parties with probably twenty people gathered round.

On the second floor were three bedrooms—a large master bedroom with a "dressing room" connected by French doors. The dressing room had a separate door to the hall, and it became for us a fourth bedroom. There was a second large middle bedroom and a somewhat smaller bedroom at the back of the house. These rooms opened to one side of a hall.

On the opposite side of the hall there were doors to the attic stairway, a linen closet, the back stairway, and the bathroom. Between the bathroom and the front bedroom there was a banister overlooking the front staircase and first floor hall. And so, there was a bedroom for my parents and one bedroom for the three girls, and two bedrooms for six boys. In fact, there were six boys only for a brief time. Soon after, Mickey was born and Brud and Jim left for the Navy.

The bathroom fixtures were original with the house. There was a clothes chute behind a small door in the wall between the toilet and sink where you could dispatch dirty clothing and bedding to the basement laundry room. The bathtub on the opposite side of the room was enormous, wide, deep, and long. Jack, Bob, and I took our baths together in groups of two or three when we were all pre- teens. The tub was so long that if you were under 5′ 5″ you could lie down entirely in it.

When Bob and Jack were teenagers, Jack, who was about five foot-tall at the time, had the habit of lying face-down in the tub and letting his body float. And so, one day Jack was floating face down in the bathtub. Bob entered the bathroom, thought Jack had drowned, and in a single motion lifted him out of the tub and laid him on his back on the floor. Of course, Jack had not heard Bob enter the bathroom and was, well, astonished is not the word for it! This became one of the often-repeated family stories.

There was a huge attic — one, big open space except for a brick chimney in the middle. The roof was probably 15 feet at the highest point. There was also a deep full basement. That was the house as built for the gentry.

We, however, were not gentry. We were a large, working-class, Irish-Catholic family with eight children ranging from a 13-year-old to a 6-month-old (me). Child number nine (Mickey) arrived around 4 years later. My father, a plumber by trade, was an all-around skilled tradesman. Partly because of the size of our family, partly because of my mother's sense of modernity, and partly because of my father's skill, and certainly because of my parents' willingness to work, 7736 S. Union got a serious makeover.

My father screened in the front porch with wooden framed screen panels that could be installed in the spring and removed and stored in the fall. That gave us a place to sit after dinner during Chicago's very hot summers, and where you could play or sit and read or just hang out during the school vacation.

The front parlor remained the parlor. As was the custom, no one sat in there except for company. The dining room became a "back parlor," our actual sitting room.

One of my abiding memories of my father was his sitting in that room next to the radio after dinner with his quart of beer. Those were evenings when he did not go out to a meeting. He belonged to a dozen organizations, primarily the plumber's union, but also the Veterans of Foreign Wars, The Loyal Order of Hibernians, The Holy Name Society, and others. To attend these meetings he took the streetcar. We sometimes had a car, but my father never took it out except for Sunday drives.

The music room became the dining room where we all ate our evening meal together. My father enlarged the doorway between the music room and kitchen so that the music room became almost an alcove (albeit a very large alcove) off the kitchen. It contained only a table and chairs large enough to accommodate all of us. In fact, there were not 11 chairs. On the side of the table nearest the wall there was a board supported by a chair at each end where four of the younger kids sat with Mickey in a highchair next to my mother.

It was at that dining room table where each of the older siblings was assigned to fill the plate of a younger sibling and where I became Norrine's boy. Breakfast was always simple—coffee, toast, Corn Flakes, sometimes oatmeal (on very cold mornings)—eaten on the fly or at the kitchen table. I do not remember a time when I did not drink coffee in the morning.

Very soon after we bought the house, my father converted the closet off the kitchen into a half-bath so my mother did not have to climb the stairs to the bathroom during the day. No one used that bathroom to get ready to leave the house in the morning; we all used the second-floor bathroom. Since we all left for work or school between 7:45 and 8:45 in the morning, there was not a lot of waiting in line, but you did not dawdle in the bathroom.

The back stairs were never used as a stairway. They were used as sort of a pantry and storage space for various and sundry. At the top of these stairs, accessible from the second- floor hall, my mother stored tomatoes, peaches, chili sauce, and grape jelly she "canned" in Mason jars every fall. That accounts for the changes made to accommodate our large family.

Modernization was a different matter. Within ten years after we moved into Union Ave, my father had torn all the ornate woodwork off the doorframes on the first floor and created arched doorways with no wood trim—the last word in modernity in the 30's and 40's. He and my mother wallpapered every room in the house and painted most of the remaining woodwork white (except for the walnut front staircase).

Most of my memories of my parent's relationship are not happy ones, but I have happy memories of them decorating a room together-- her at a table of plywood supported by sawhorses — trimming, pasting and folding the wallpaper, so it could be handled easily. Him on a ladder applying the paper to the wall, sliding it into place so it would match, smoothing it against the wall with a specially made brush, and trimming the paper at the ceiling and baseboard. They seemed quite content and happy with each other.

World War II ended ten years after we moved into Union Avenue and the service men were returning and getting married. This was the beginning of the "baby boom" and there was an enormous housing shortage. My father raised the roof on both sides of the house creating dormers that made it possible to put rooms into the attic. He created a three-room apartment — kitchen, sitting room, bedroom, and a full bath.

The apartment did not have its own entrance, however. You had to come in the front door, climb the front stairs, walk to the back of the second-floor hall and up the attic stairs to get to the apartment. That made it less private than one wished, and my mother was prone to getting involved in whatever was going on in *her* house. Norrine, Brud, and Bob all lived there for a short time when they were newly married, but they moved out as soon as they could.

As my older brothers and sisters began to leave home, my mother converted what was the original dining room back into a dining room. The music room became a small television room with just a two-seat couch and an easy chair. We brought additional chairs in from the kitchen if they were needed. We ate all our meals in the kitchen.

The basement on Union Avenue was one damned scary place. You opened the basement door off the first-floor hall and stepped out onto the basement stairs landing. There was a bare 60-watt light bulb on the landing, but to your right you were looking down into the dark at the bottom of the stairs. You descended and turned right into the dark passage between the coal bin and the furnace. You walked further into the dark and turned right again into the dark passage in front of the coal furnace. There you turned on another bare light bulb hanging from the rafters. Even with these lights turned on there were still areas that were dark, places you could not see into.

The furnace had two doors — the top door for adding coal to the fire and the bottom door for removing ashes. The bottom door had a damper which could be opened, giving the fire more oxygen and making it burn faster and hotter or closed to deprive the fire of oxygen and make it burn slower. There were asbestos-covered hot air ducts coming off the top of the furnace and running all around the basement ceiling and to the floors above. These ducts made for places with more shadows than light even with the light turned on.

There was no light bulb in the coal bin. At the beginning of winter, the coal filled the bin right up to the door opening into the furnace area and you could see by the light in front of the furnace. As the coal got used up, you had to walk further and further back into a nearly pitch-black space at the back of the coal bin. You were entirely cut off from the family upstairs — it seemed like from the entire rest of the world. There would have to be a real racket in the basement for anyone upstairs to hear it. A common source of merriment among family members was hearing one of the younger boys racing up the basement stairs after tending the furnace. No one had to explain what the joke was.

Every day during the winter one of the boys, starting at about age 12, tended the furnace before school in the morning and once again after school. "Tending the fire" meant adding coal to the left or right side of the fire pit depending on where the fire had burned longer and the coal had begun to turn to ash. As the fire spread to the new coal, it became a red-hot mass and the former hot coals burned out and turned to ash. You "shook down" the ashes by agitating the grate that the fire rested on by working a handle next to the furnace that was attached to the grate.

If the ash pit was full, or nearly full you shoveled the ashes out and deposited them in buckets (old 10-gallon paint containers) kept next to the furnace. One of the boys took ashes to the alley and dumped them next to the garbage cans on Saturday. The garbage men picked up the ashes with shovels and tossed them into the garbage truck (or horse-drawn wagon before World War II). Additionally, the fire needed to be "banked" every night before bed. You shook it down, added more coal than usual, emptied the ashes if necessary, and nearly closed the damper for a long winter's rest.

There were a number of ways this could go wrong: If you added too much coal (or not enough), or allowed the ash pit to get too full, or turned down the damper too much, the fire would go out. Then you started over with newspaper, kindling wood and a match—adding a little coal at a time to coax a coal fire into existence.

One morning when I was in high school, I went down to the fire and it was out, and I decided to take a little short cut. My father kept a blowtorch in the basement, a standard piece of equipment of the plumbing trade at the time, and there was always some unused gasoline in it. And so, I just added coal to the furnace and doused it with what I thought was a tiny bit of gasoline. I lit a match, bent over to throw it into the furnace door, and there was an explosion that knocked me several feet back against the wall behind me.

I thought my mother must have heard it, or that it might have blown the dust that gathered in the heating ducts into the first-floor rooms, and I was sure I would catch hell. But I didn't hear anything from upstairs, and so I fixed the fire starting with paper and kindling wood as I should have done in the first place and went up upstairs. My mother was oblivious to the fact that I just came close to killing myself and maybe burning the house down. My eyebrows were actually a little singed, but she didn't notice.

Next to the furnace toward the back of the basement (closest to the back yard) was an un-insulated steel hot water tank behind a small coal-fired hot water furnace. The big furnace heated water during the winter, but in summer you had to build a fire in the small furnace every time you needed hot water—which was on Monday mornings for "the wash," on Saturdays for baths, and any other time during the week that someone needed a bath. We heated water on the kitchen stove for dish washing. My father and older brothers shaved using cold water on normal workday mornings.

By the 1950s we had a gas hot-water heater in the basement and so we had hot water all the time. We also had a new coal furnace with a fan to force the hot air into the house and a thermostat in the dining room. The damper on the furnace was opened and closed by an electric motor as the thermostat demanded more or less heat. But it was still a coal furnace that needed attention three or more times every day.

There is something very Jungian about my experience of that dark basement on Union Avenue. When I was doing talk therapy with a shrink at about age 50, I related an experience I had had in the basement on Union Avenue: I was at least 12—old enough to be tending the furnace. I was coming out of the coal bin with a shovel full of coal walking toward the open fire door of the furnace when I remembered something, and I said, aloud, I think, "Well, *that* explains everything!" — *that* being the thought that had come to me between the coal bin and the fire door. But I do not remember what that thought was.

The psychiatrist who was, in a word, non-directive, suddenly seemed to awaken from his slumbers and wanted to know more about that. "How old was I?" (At least 12 — old enough to be tending the furnace.) "How often had I remembered this incident since?" (Probably once or twice a year every year since then.) "What happened after that?" (I don't remember. I think I had stopped thinking about it by the time I finished tending the furnace and got to the top of the stairs.) I asked him if he could help me remember through hypnosis. He said he could try, but he did not think that would be wise.

I have always suspected that this incident had something to do with my relationship with my mother. That would put the incident somewhere into my teen years when I began to see that my relationship with her was more complicated and troubled than her relationships with my siblings. Also, being afraid in the basement was no part of this memory, making me believe that I was probably at least 13 or 14.

This psychiatrist was not a particularly gifted therapist. He didn't claim to be. When I asked whether he was Freudian,

Jungian, Adlerian, or whatever, he answered, "I'm a biologist. I have a nice medication here to treat your depression, and if you want to go on with these talk sessions, fine. But if you won't take the pills, see someone else. Talk therapy helps a little; medications help a lot. Combined you get a lot plus a little." I've come to believe he was right although I've seen therapists for short periods since with good results when the Dark Night seemed to be getting the upper hand.

My mother's week. Monday was wash-day. The back of the basement (closest to the back yard) was partially cut off from the furnace area by a brick wall — the foundation for the house chimney. Behind the chimney were washtubs and a wringer washer. To one side against the wall there was a very old gas stove. It was heavily enameled — cream colored with light green trim, probably very fashionable in the 1920s. The stove was on legs. The oven was on the right, positioned as if on top of a table, and the burners were on the left at tabletop level. There were no pilots. Lighting the oven and each burner required a match and some dexterity to keep from getting your fingers burned by the igniting gas.

My mother used this stove to boil water to make starch for my father's and the older boys' dress shirts, her cotton house-dresses and aprons, and whatever blouses, and so on of the girls that needed starching. In the corner opposite the stove there were about six stairs that led to a landing at ground level and a door out into the back yard. To the left of the washtubs and back toward an area behind the furnaces a barrel stood under the clothes chute. Clothes put into the

53

chute from the second-floor bathroom fell into this barrel. There was a second opening to the chute on the first floor for kitchen towels and whatever soiled clothes accumulated on the first floor.

On Monday mornings my mother and father went to 6:30 a.m. mass at St. Leo Church. After mass, my father would make a fire in the hot water furnace before leaving for work on the Halsted Street streetcar. Before leaving for school one of the boys would string clothesline in the back yard.

After the rest of us were off to work or school my mother would read the *Chicago Tribune* with her coffee. The *Tribune* was a very Republican paper, but it was the best newspaper covering national news. Then she would descend into the basement where she did eight or more washers full of clothing. She emptied the clothes barrel onto the concrete floor and sorted the sheets and clothing. She filled the washer with hot water and, with a paring knife, sliced shavings from a bar of brown Fels Naphtha or American Family soap into the washer full of hot soapy water. She added her first load clothes into the washer and turned on the agitator.

She filled the two washtubs with clear cold water. After 15 minutes or so she would take the clothes from the washer and put them through the wringer into the first tub of clear-cold water and add another load to the washer. Then she would put the clothes from the first clear water washtub through the wringer into the second clear water tub, and finally wring the clothes into a basket giving her nice clean, well-rinsed and well-wrung clothing ready to hang out to dry.

She repeated this routine the seven or eight times necessary to wash all the clothes, changing the hot soapy water in the washer and the clear water in the washtubs as necessary. Once the process had produced a basket of washed and rinsed clothes she carried the basket to the back yard, hung the clothes onto the clotheslines using wooden clothespins, and raised the clotheslines with eight- or nine-foot wooden clothes-poles.

Things that needed to be starched needed an additional step. She dipped the garment or the part that needed starch (only the front, the collar, and the cuffs of men's white shirts for example) into the just boiled starch, held it for a minute letting the excess drip back into the starch container, and when the fabric had cooled enough—not nearly cool enough for anyone who was not used to this procedure—she wrung the starch out by hand and added these items to the baskets of clothes to be hung.

Numerous decisions were involved here. White items were washed first when the water was cleanest and hottest. Dyes were more likely to "run" in these days so certain items could not be washed in the same water. When the soapy water and the rinsing water needed changing was another judgment call.

During the winter and on rainy Mondays, my mother would hang the clothes on lines permanently strung around the basement ceiling wherever possible—in front of the furnace, between the washtubs and the back wall, and in the space behind the furnace near the clothes chute. Although she had all these jobs in progress there were moments of downtime when she sat in a chair next to the gas stove *and said a rosary.* I am not making this up.

My mother came up to the kitchen around noon on washdays. Those of us in elementary school came home for lunch. We mostly took care of our own lunch, bologna or "spiced ham" (kind of like Spam only sliced lunch meat) sandwiches. She would send one of us up to the "High-Low" on Halsted Street for dinner items. We had an hour for lunch and there was plenty of time. High-Low was among the first "supermarkets" where you could buy vegetables, meat, bread, milk, canned foods, and household cleaning supplies all in one store. My mother would have her lunch and listen to soap operas on the radio--"One Man's Family," "Ma Perkins," and "A Brighter Day".

When we left for school, my mother would descend once again into the basement to finish the wash. She came upstairs around three to take a bath and change into a clean house-dress for when my father came home, and to start dinner. She did take a daily nap, but probably not on Monday. One or more of us children would take down the wash and the clothesline after school.

Tuesday was ironing day. My mother ironed in the kitchen, first dampening the clothes on the kitchen table, rolling them up in tight rolls, and putting them in the basket. She ironed several starched, white dress shirts that my father and older brothers wore on weekends. In fact, my father wore a suit and white shirt to go to work on the Halsted Street streetcar.

He changed into a one piece "coverall" in his little "office" in the basement of the Health Department where he was the in-house plumber maintaining the washrooms and laboratories throughout the eight-story building on Hubbard Street near Halsted. Since he only wore his white shirt going and coming from work, he probably wore the same white shirt all week.

There was no "wash and wear" fabric in those days and nearly every item of clothing needed at least a lick and a promise with a hot iron. All the while my mother ironed, she listened to the radio—Arthur Godfrey around 10 a. m. followed by the soaps well into the afternoon. Arthur Godfrey was a pioneer in a genre of radio talk shows that appealed to housewives. He called himself the "Old Redhead" and his voice dripped with charm. In his private life he is reputed to have been a bastardly megalomaniac, and the 1957 movie "A Face in the Crowd" is widely believed to be based on him.

My mother's Mondays and Tuesdays convey two impressions of her. The first impression is that she was responsible, dependable, hard-working, and determined that although she had a large family, her children were turned out looking great in neat, clean cloths and they were expected to meet the world unapologetically and with their chins up. That impression is correct.

The second impression — concerning the daily mass and the rosaries — is that she was sanctimonious. That is decidedly incorrect. She had a deep, uncomplicated faith, but she would never be described as sanctimonious. While observing her in her daily interactions, religiosity would be the last thing to enter your mind. Down-to-earth would be more likely. When she prayed "for *us* sinners," (part of the "Hail Mary" which one recites 53 times in praying a rosary) she no doubt included herself among the sinners, but she wasn't sappy about it. She too met the world unapologetically and with her chin up.

On Wednesday, Thursday, and Friday my mother took care of business. Considering the monumental amount of work my mother did raising nine children and keeping a big house, she engaged in a surprising number of civic and parish activities. She "canvassed" our precinct for the Democratic Party before every election. That is, she carried political literature from door to door and urged people to get out and vote Democratic. And, she was a Democratic judge at the polls on election days.

She sold poppies for the VFW (Veterans of Foreign Wars) on Memorial Day. She sold religious goods in the parish clubhouse during "Mission Weeks" when priests from a religious order—Jesuits or Franciscans, for example—delivered special sermons and instructions on five weeknights for the men of the parish followed by a week for the women of the parish. On top of all of this she attended Altar and Rosary meetings and met regularly for coffee with neighborhood women in someone's kitchen.

And she had nerve. She once told me that during the height of the Great Depression a man came to our house one day to shut off the gas because of an unpaid bill. In desperation she said to him, "If you touch that valve (the valve that he was about to lock shut) I'll put an Irish curse on you!" She was, of course, not Irish, but who ever heard of a Czech curse? She said she "scared the crap out of him." He left, with the gas still on.

Then, she sent one of us kids up to Dix Hardware Store, where you could pay your utility bills, and paid a few dollars on the bill to keep the gas company at bay till better times. That was her—gutsy. But she also attended mass daily and said the rosary while doing the wash. In fact, she kept a rosary under her pillow for odd moments of wakefulness during the night. You did not know my mother long without knowing the gutsy part. Not one in a hundred people who knew her casually would have known about the daily mass and rosary.

Although not pious, we were very observant Catholics. We were strict believers in Catholic doctrine as spelled out by the priests at St. Leo Church. We believed we would go to Hell if we died "in mortal sin." Missing Mass on Sunday and eating meat on Friday were mortal sins. Any sexual act except for vaginal intercourse between a man and woman married by a Catholic priest was a mortal sin. Any form of contraception was a mortal sin. A second marriage after a divorce was not considered valid, and so couples in such marriages were "living in sin."

Everyone went to Mass every Sunday and on the six holy days of obligation such as Christmas on December 25 and All Saints Day on November 1. We did not eat meat on Fridays. One Friday my mother noticed that there was beef stock in the Campbell's Cream of Mushroom soup that she used in her tuna casserole (a Friday night staple) and she sent me to the parish rectory to ask if it would be all right to eat the casserole. If the priest had said no, we would no doubt have had macaroni and cheese for dinner. (He said it would be ok.) We "gave up" things (chocolate, for example) for the season of Lent. I don't think anyone ever made it through the entire 46 days, but we started out earnestly.

When there were a lot of us in school, we were home on Good Friday, and we sometimes set out to "keep the silence" between noon and three o'clock when Jesus is believed to have hung on the cross. This usually turned into a lot of silly sign language, hilarity, and "breaking the silence" within the first hour. That was us — observant, but not sappy about it.

My mother and father had given us a good home, fed and clothed us, set the right example for us, sent us to Catholic schools to be educated, seen to it that we performed our religious duties, hustled us off to Confession regularly, gave us a few coins for the collection, and never allowed us to miss Mass. I think the first time I noticed that Bob and I had reached a fork in the road was when I realized he did not always go to Mass when he left for church on Sunday morning. How that was possible was beyond my comprehension.

Chapter 6.

THE NEIGHBORHOOD

Alleys. Chicago streets are laid out on a near-perfect grid. In our neighborhood, as in most Chicago neighborhoods, north-south streets had names—Union Avenue, Halsted Street, and so on. East-west streets were numbered-79th Street, 80th Street, and so on. The numbered streets were called side-streets. Alleys, concrete roads barely two car widths wide, ran between most north-south streets. There are, in fact, 19,000 miles of alleys in Chicago.

Our house on Union Avenue on the Southside of Chicago had a backyard, and behind the yard was an alley. My father sometimes owned an eight- or ten-year- old used car that stayed in the garage except for Sundays when he took the kids out for a ride—often to Hines Veterans Hospital to visit Uncle George.

The alley was a busy place. Pedestrians took short cuts through alleys and children played in the alleys behind their homes. Every morning the milkman made deliveries from the alley to his customers' back door. When I was very young, the iceman still came down our alley two or three times a week delivering ice to the few neighbors who did not yet have electric refrigerators. We always had an electric refrigerator.

Eugene O'Neill's play entitled, "The Iceman Cometh," was a wry reference to an inside joke among housewives. An icemen needed to enter the kitchen of the homes that he delivered to so that he could he put the block of ice, which he carried on his shoulder, into the customer's ice-box. Icemen were reputed to have sex with some of the housewives, and neighboring housewives would call to one another, "Is the iceman coming?"

Garbage men came down the alley once a week — lifting and dumping our garbage cans (fifty-gallon drums) into a horse-drawn wagon or truck and shoveling up the spillage and the ashes from our coal furnace that we had dumped next to our garbage cans. In my earliest memories, certainly up to the start of World War II, the milk and garbage wagons were horse-drawn. Later they became motor vehicles and eventually the garbage trucks added loading apparatus so the garbage containers could be emptied nearer the ground level. Milk trucks disappeared as shopping habits of American city dwellers changed.

Occasionally a ragman came up the alley pushing or pulling a cart — no horses, no motors — and shouting melodically, "rags o line" ("Rags and old iron"). Housewives sent children out with their offerings of rags and scraps of metal such as parts of broken tools and appliances. Very occasionally, a man would come up the alley with an apparatus strapped to his back and ringing a bell that told householders he was there to sharpen knives and tools. When he had a customer, he would set the apparatus down on the ground. It was about waist high and had a grinding wheel at the top that he turned with a crank or a foot pedal to sharpen the tools.

The Rock Island Railroad came through our neighborhood running parallel to Union Avenue and three blocks east of us. The tracks were elevated but there was not the usual embankment that you see along many elevated railroad lines going through a city. Instead, the landfill the tracks lay on was encased on each side by concrete walls that stood about two stories high. In some parts of the city these concrete walls were known as "the escarpment."

We referred to the walls, the tracks, and all simply as "the tracks." Seventy-Eighth Street ran under the tracks through a tunnel that we referred to as "the elevation." You went "through the elevation" to get to "the other side of the tracks." There was a Rock Island station at street level under the tracks on the far side of the elevation.

Because the Rock Island tracks interrupted the grid scheme of Chicago streets, the first street on "the other side of the tracks" had no alley behind it, and the people who lived there put their garbage cans in front of their houses.

They were very poor and I grew up associating the absence of alleys, and garbage cans in front of the houses, with poverty. On our side of the tracks there was a strip of grass about twenty yards wide and three blocks long called Lyle Park. This grass was a favorite place for kids to play. My limited (very limited) experience playing football and baseball was in this park.

All of the houses on our block were built between 1880 and the 1920s. They were a collection of stone, brick, and frame buildings. My world, before I started high school, was bordered by the Rock Island Railroad tracks three blocks east, Halsted Street two blocks west, 80th Street two blocks south, and 76th Street two blocks north. Since there a was a Rock Island Railroad station at 78th Street, and both 79th Street and Halsted Street were main thoroughfares with streetcar lines, we were ideally located for transportation to downtown Chicago, that was about 10 miles northeast.

Streetcars and streets. Downtown was about an hour away by streetcar (with one transfer) and 40 minutes by train. This probably accounted for the fact that the original family breadwinners in our neighborhood (nearly all men, of course) worked downtown in white-collar jobs and were solidly middle-class. By the mid-1930s there was a broad spectrum of owners and renters including blue-collar workers like the Finns.

Emerald Avenue lay between us and Halsted Street.

St. Leo Catholic Church, its rectory, community hall, and grammar school took up about one third of the west side of the block. The convent with its walled garden was on the east side of the street, across from the school. The back wall of the convent and the eight-foot brick wall of the convent garden were right on the alley and directly behind our house.

My brothers Jack and Bob and Ed Scully, Donald Clancy, and Donny Lynch were around my age and the alley behind our house was our playground. We played "Kick the Can," endlessly it seems, but also "Red Rover," "Cops and Robbers," and "Cowboys and Indians." Neighborhood girls joined us at times. We sometimes played baseball and on more than one occasion a nun from the convent came out the kitchen door and took a turn at bat, but she never ran the bases.

Gangways. Between most houses in our neighborhood there were narrow sidewalks running from the front sidewalk to the alley behind the house. We called them "gangways." Everyone knew which neighbors did not object to your walking "down their gangway" on the way to church, school, or to Halsted Street to shop or catch a streetcar. On Sunday morning there would be upwards of twenty people walk down our gangway to the alley behind our house, down the alley, and down Clancy's gangway to Emerald Avenue where St. Leo church was located. That made St. Leo church and school just two or three minutes from our back door.

Most houses and buildings in this square quarter mile were single-family residences and "two-flats" that had one apartment on the first floor and a second apartment on the second floor. Houses and two-flats were built no more than ten yards apart. On Lowe Avenue, the street between us and the tracks, there was a tiny Protestant church; its parsonage was on the corner of our block on Union Avenue. Across from the parsonage there was also an enormous 14-room mansion surrounded by expansive well-cared for lawns. On the next block south of us on Union Avenue there was a Masonic Temple with a porch roof supported by four two-story columns.

A block north of us on Union Avenue there was another huge house with a driveway and covered portico designed to protect passengers alighting from carriages in rain or falling snow; and just three doors from us there was a low red brick residence that might have been designed by Frank Lloyd Wright (it wasn't). It was surrounded by wide manicured lawns. It was owned by the Ferns who owned a mortuary at 79th and Emerald. We always referred to Fern's as the "Protestant Undertakers."

Scattered through the neighborhood were several three-story red brick apartment buildings built around courtyards with a dozen or more apartments facing each courtyard. Landings on the stairways in these buildings were extra wide to accommodate carrying a casket in the days when the departed were "waked" in their own living rooms.

Movie theaters and shops. There were two movie theaters just three blocks from us on Halsted Street. The Capital was a big theater with a large lobby, a big balcony, marble staircases, and 'the works' in terms of movie palace décor. The price of tickets was 25 cents for a double feature, one of them "first run." The Cosmo was a very modest little movie theater across the street from the Capital. The price of a ticket was 14 cents for a double feature—always "B" movies. There were two "Popcorn Stores"—one next to the Capital in a regular storefront, and one next to the Cosmo in a tiny shack. There was both a White Castle and a Wimpey's— hamburger joints, forerunners to McDonalds. Wimpey's was named after a very fat male character in the comic strip called "Popeye the Sailor Man."

The south terminal of the Halsted Street streetcar line was between 79th and 80th Streets. The "streetcar barns" were a few doors from the Capital. The streetcar barns were not actually buildings. They were a large lot where streetcars were switched from the southbound tracks to the northbound tracks for their run back downtown.

There was a big Walgreens Drug Store at the corner of 79th and Halsted with a large lunch counter, and there was an independently owned pharmacy (The Scientific Pharmacy) with a small soda fountain at 78th and Halsted. My sisters Mary and Joan were "soda jerks" there when they were in high school. I would go in, order a soda, hand Mary or Joan a quarter, and they would hand me a nickel and two dimes change. There was no cash register at the soda counter, just a dish to put proceeds and make change.

There were men's clothing stores and women's dress shops, a Chinese laundry that did men's shirts almost exclusively, a tiny shop (NuMode) that sold nothing but women's nylon stockings — an item of apparel that had just become available after World War II. There were restaurants and an impressive bank building, The Mutual National Bank. My mother had a checking account there.

There were three butcher shops, a vegetable market, a fish monger, two "supermarkets" (High-Lo and Consumers), at least four taverns — Sterling, Burkhart's, The Three Pats, and New York Liquors. Sterling and New York Liquors each had a carryout liquor store attached. There was a photography studio, a chocolate shop (homemade chocolates made on the premises by Mr. and Mrs. Driscoll, the proprietors), and a used car lot.

There was a public library, three mortuaries (Quinlin's and Sheehy's patronized by Catholics and Fern's patronized by Protestants), "The Vogue" that sold knickknacks and greeting cards, a baby carriage and nursery furnishings store, an insurance office, a real estate office, a currency exchange, the Rock Island station, Ogelsby public elementary school and playground, Leo Lynch Cleaners that also rented formal ware, Knight's Florist, a Sinclair Gas Station, a cigar and cigarette store, and Dix Hardware store that must have had a thousand items. Mr. or Mrs. Dix went directly to the shelf for any item you asked for. You could also pay your utilities bills at Dix's.

There were two bakeries — Widen's with a full range of cakes, pies, sweet rolls, and bread — and Diebold's that sold mainly bread and bread rolls. The Diebolds were an older German couple with very thick accents. Mrs. Diebold muttered to herself in German continuously and neighborhood lore had it that she had been shell-shocked back in Germany during World War I.

There were two barbershops, a beauty parlor, a "shoemaker" (you had soles and heels replaced on shoes in those days), and a paint and wallpaper store (with a taxidermy rendering of the owner's departed German Shepherd in the window). In the floors above the stores and shops on Halsted and 79th Streets there were lawyers, doctors and dentist offices.

Above Walgreens there was NuPhone, a telephone answering service where Norrine and my mother each worked at one time or another, Fox Secretarial College, and Local Loan, a commercial loan company that would lend money to individuals with poor credit ratings at high rates of interest. These were the granddaddies of today's payday loan companies.

There was a wide assortment of denizens on our block as well. Dolans lived across the street from us. He traded in livestock at the Chicago Stock Yards, and he drove an enormous Lincoln. His children went away to college (making them a one-of-a-kind family in our neighborhood). I have a vivid memory of seeing their son Paul walking from his car to the house in a white tennis outfit. It may be the only time I ever saw him. It's certainly the only time I saw anyone in tennis togs in our neighborhood. I ran errands for Mrs. Dolan when I was in grade school. They had genuine Tiffany lamps. She was very generous—a twenty-five cent tip which was practically unheard of.

Reverend Babbin, the pastor of the tiny Protestant Church on Lowe Avenue, lived in the house next to Dolans. I never laid eyes on him or his wife or his children—presuming he had them. Ferns (the Protestant undertaker) owned a house three doors down from us. I would frequently see Mrs. Fern tending her perfectly groomed lawn during the summer. I don't believe she ever spoke to any of the neighbors, maybe a smile. *Noblesse obliges*. Galls lived next to the Ferns. He was a dentist. They had one daughter. Although they passed our house frequently, I do not think we ever said more than hello to them. They were Protestants.

Scullys lived across the alley. He owned an insurance firm and also had a concrete business. Mrs. Scully's father had been lieutenant-governor of Illinois. They had a large house across the street from St. Leo Church. They were Catholic. They had an enormous elk head over their fireplace in the living room, presumably a trophy from Mr. Scully's hunting in the north woods of Wisconsin. Scullys had five children. Their oldest boy became a doctor and was our family physician by the time I was in high school. My mother was a close friend of Mrs. Scully.

Morrisseys lived two doors down. They were good friends of my parents. He had a nondescript white-collar job with the Rock Island Railroad. They lived in Mrs. Morrissey's family home. Annie, Mrs. Morrissey's sister, never married and she lived there as well. The grandfather was very old and sat in a chair in the living room dressed in a suit and tie staring into space day in and day out. When I was six or seven and went to Morrissey's on an errand for my mother, I was always told to go in and say hello to Grandpa. I did as I was told; he always seemed startled and nodded at me, and that was that.

The McDermotts lived further down the block. He owned a butcher shop on Halsted Street. I worked for him during my last year in high school. There was a dozen or more people who walked past our house every evening around six coming home from work (office work judging from their apparel) on the Rock Island or the Halsted Streetcar. I never knew their names. They lived in the one or two boardinghouses further up the block. One was a slight dark complected man who wore a Zoot suit (wide padded shoulders, wide lapels, tight waist, and baggy trousers pegged at the ankles). He was rumored to be a Filipino, which was the occasion for some dark allusions to the neighborhood "changing."

The Lynches lived across the alley. He owned a tavern, but they lived in a rented apartment, and they always seemed poor. I always felt vaguely that the old man was violent. Donny was a little younger than I but he was often part of a collection of kids who played in the alley. Then there were the Schumakes. He was a carpenter who worked every day but drank up most of his pay. They lived in a rented top-floor apartment of a two-flat and they were very poor. There always seemed to be something "Appalachian-poor" about them, although I think both parents were born in Chicago.

Downstairs in the same two-flat were the Clancy's. He was hopelessly alcoholic. They were very poor but somehow Mrs. Clancy held it together and their children seemed pretty upstanding. Their youngest boy was my brother Bob's age. He wanted to become a priest, but instead he joined an order of brothers because he did not cut the mustard at the seminary. Twenty years later when the supply of boys entering the seminary was drying up, Donald did become a priest.

And of course, there were the six or eight priests who lived in the St. Leo Rectory and twenty-six nuns who lived in the convent just behind us — twenty-four of them were teachers, three in each of the eight grades, plus the school principal, and the cook/housekeeper—the one who sometimes took turns at bat.

The only Jewish family in our neighborhood owned the baby-carriage store on Halsted Street and lived above the store. They had a boy about my age whom I would see on rare occasions in the tiny back yard behind the store as I went down the alley behind the church. I never spoke to him. I do not believe our eyes ever met. I think even at a very early age that I knew he had a life somewhere outside of our neighborhood.

Changing demography. My mother sold the house on Union Avenue in 1958, and my mother, Jack, and I moved into a two-bedroom apartment just south of 79th Street and west of Halsted. More than the fact that just the three of us were living in this huge house, this move was prompted by the changing demography of the city—of the nation really.

Just before World War I, "Negroes" from the Jim Crow South were migrating to cities in the North and West as part of the First Great Migration. A Second Great Migration occurred before and after World War II. By 1958, Black families had moved into St. Leo parish, and the neighborhood had become totally Black by 1970 when Jesse Jackson's Southern Christian Leadership Conference bought The Capital Theater as their headquarters and conference venue.

Chapter 7.

"A DAY THAT WILL LIVE IN INFAMY"

I turned six in October of 1941. Less than two months later Japan attacked the United States Pacific fleet anchored in Pearl Harbor in Hawaii. The attack started at 7:55 a.m. on Sunday, December 7. That would have been about noon in Chicago.

On a typical Sunday morning in December of 1941 my mother and father would have been at 6:30 a.m. mass at St. Leo. They would have come home and read the *Chicago Tribune* and the *Chicago Times* which they bought from one of the McCann boys who were St. Leo parishioners and had "the franchise" on after-mass paper sales outside St. Leo Church on Sundays.

Around 8:00 a.m. my parents would have begun to get the younger kids up and out to 9:00 o'clock mass and they would have begun to fix Sunday dinner. My father peeled potatoes and did whatever other preparations of vegetables as was necessary. There was always a tray of celery, green onions, radishes, and sometimes olives with Sunday dinner. You put salt on your dinner plate for dipping them.

My mother would have gotten the meat ready for dinner, and once it was in the oven, she would have begun to make a chocolate cake with white icing and Jello for the Sunday evening meal that was served around 6:00 p. m. Our Sunday evening meal was always sandwiches, cake and Jello.

My father would have finished earlier than my mother and repaired to the living room to listen to the radio and continue reading the paper. As my mother got the meal on the table, he would make the gravy and slice the meat. Those Sunday mornings with my mother and father working together to get the Sunday afternoon meal ready were times I remember them being happy together.

By noon, Mary, Jack, Joan, Bob, and I would have been to 9:00 Mass, the children's Mass. Except for Jack, who went to Gompers School for Crippled Children, we were all students at St. Leo Grammar School, and we sat with our class in the church. Jack probably sat with Bob's class. After Mass, we would come home and read the comic sections of *The Chicago Tribune* and *The Chicago Sun Times* — "Dick Tracy," "Bringing Up Father," "Annie," and "Blondie." We always called the comics "the funnies." The older children, Norrine, Brud, and Jim, were out of school and would have been at 12:00 p.m. Mass. Dinner was served around one p.m. when they got home from church, and all eleven of us sat down together to eat — Mickey in his highchair next to my mother.

There had been two years of worry about whether the U. S. would enter the war that had started in Europe in 1939.

We had entered World War I a few years after it started in Europe, and we were edging toward going to war in Europe once again. The news of the Japanese attack would have come over the radio. My father would have heard it on the radio sometime between noon and one o'clock and I imagine there would have been mayhem — my father cursing the "goddamned Japs" and my mother in tears. No doubt they were both thinking of my oldest brothers who were 17 and 16. They would be going to war. I can only imagine the anger, heartache, and fear. An attack from Japan was totally unexpected. *Surprise* attack was a colossal understatement.

I don't remember anyone comforting me. I think my mother and father probably did, but I only remember that some country was dropping bombs on *us*, and I thought bombs would soon start falling on Chicago, on our neighborhood, on our house. At some point I ran to the attic thinking irrationally that that was the safest place. Or perhaps I didn't think safety was possible and what I wanted to do was hide and the attic seemed like the best place.

I have been terrified only twice in my life — scared about as often as anyone, I suppose, but terrified only twice. Once when I was about 10, sleeping between my brothers Bob and Jack in our shared double bed in the back bedroom on Union Avenue, I had sort of a dream, but it was not a dream of something happening; there were no people in it. I just became aware of the vastness of the universe. I climbed over Bob and ran to my parents' bedroom and climbed into bed with them. The other occasion was that early Sunday afternoon in December of 1941 when I thought bombs would soon fall on our house and I wanted to hide.

Within the next few days my brother Jim, who was only 16, joined the Navy using a bogus birth certificate probably with my parents' connivance. In fact, my father got phony birth certificates for several of my older brothers and sisters so they could go to work below the legal age to leave school or to be employed.

He would simply go to the Bureau of Records at City Hall and ask for a birth certificate for James Stephen Finn, for example, wink at the clerk and say, "You probably will not be able to find it." The clerk would come back to the counter and say, "No I can't find it. You will need to swear an affidavit." My father would fill out an affidavit saying his son James Stephen Finn was born on January 21, 1925, and *voila!* James Stephen Finn was now 17 rather than 16.

Jim served on a ship in the Pacific. He never said anything about where he had been or what he did in the war, or if he did, I never heard it. Brud joined the Navy about a year later. He went to Great Lakes Naval Base 40 or 50 miles north of Chicago. While there he was diagnosed with a stomach ulcer and he served out his tour but he never left Great Lakes.

The war ended in Europe on May 8, 1945 and in Japan four months later — after we had dropped atomic bombs on Hiroshima and Nagasaki on August 8 and 9, 1945. America, during any of the wars since then, —Korea, Viet Nam, or the recent wars in the Middle East—has not been anything like America during World War II. Every unmarried, able-bodied male between the ages of 18 and 29 was drafted. Toward the end of the war, they were taking 30-year-old married men with children. Seminarians studying for the Catholic priesthood were exempt from the draft and they were sent to monasteries outside cities during summer vacation, because draft-aged men walking the streets in civilian clothing would have caused enormous resentment.

We, like many of our neighbors, kept chickens in our back yard because of the food shortage. My father would kill the chickens with a hatchet over the washtubs in the basement, remove their feathers by submerging the freshly killed chicken into a big pot of boiling water on the stove where my mother made starch on washday and pulling the feathers off with his bare hands. He also made soap on the basement stove with lye and animal fat collected from beef and pork roasts and fried bacon.

Part II

THE TASTE OF AN OLIVE

Chapter 8.

ST. LEO GRAMMAR SCHOOL

I started first grade at St. Leo Grammar School at age six in September of 1941. The school was run by the Sisters of Providence. Imagine having a woman who chose to be a teacher, who lives in a community of teachers, who has no spouse or children, whose meals are prepared for her, whose household duties are shared by 24 other women, who is in bed by 10 p.m. and rises at 6 a.m. to attend Mass and receive Communion.

What a lot of time and effort could go into preparing for each teaching day. Added to that, contrary to the lore regarding corporal punishment in Catholic schools that has come into vogue in recent years, my teachers were kind and caring. Some a little more; some a little less, but all kind and caring.

Corporal punishment was allowed, but it rarely happened. Only once in eight years did I get a mild slap on the side of the head. It's a long story, and I didn't deserve it, but I knew why she did it (it was the boy ahead of me in line who had misbehaved; she simply got the wrong culprit), and so it was no big deal. In fact, I was momentarily a celebrity among my peers. "What did you do?" "Did it hurt?" "Do you think she'll tell Sister Superior?" "Are you going to tell your mother?"

First grade was pretty much about learning to read, to print the letters of the alphabet and simple words, and to write numbers and learn some addition facts. Religion instruction was limited to Sister telling us that Jesus and his Blessed Mother loved us and they wanted us to be good boys and girls. We should "love God with all our heart" — even more than we love our own mothers. I was OK with the first part, but "More than my mother?" I had certain reservations about that.

In second grade we were prepared to make our first Confession (The sacrament of Penance) and receive our First Holy Communion. That would have meant memorizing the Ten Commandments. The sixth (no adultery) and tenth (don't covet your neighbor's wife) were skated over. After all, we were only seven years old. "Religion" was mostly an admonition to love God, and not to steal, cheat, lie, or hurt others. By middle grades the nuns might have mentioned "impure thoughts" as something to be avoided, but it was left to the priests to unleash Hell's Fire and Damnation upon us.

In seventh and eighth grade we were brought over to the church for separate "girl's missions" and "boy's missions" where a priest lectured us about having "impure thoughts" and being "impure in action with yourself or others." In one sermon we were asked to consider a ball of steel as large as the earth that a butterfly came to every one-hundred years and brushed its wings against it. When that steel ball disappeared because of erosion from the butterfly's wings, eternity would just be beginning.

And there were no sissy abstractions about how the pain of hell is that "one is denied the sight of God for eternity." Hell is fire! Fire burns, and you don't get burned up. It keeps on hurting for eternity! Is what you gain from sin worth this price? This is pretty heavy shit for a twelve-year-old. As I write this, I am reminded of the sermon James Joyce reported in *A Portrait of the Artist as a Young man*. Same old, same old.

By the upper grades we began to get into more formal knowledge regarding the church. What is the difference between a "mortal" sin and a "venial" sin? What is a "holy day of obligation"? How must a holy day of obligation be observed? What is a day of fasting — and a day of abstinence? How are they observed? What are the parts of a mass - the Kyrie, Gloria, Credo, and so on? What are the parts of a cathedral — the Nave, Transept, Apse, Aisle, and so on? I got on with that very well, and I was interested in even more esoteric matters such as the difference between two types of prayer: *adoration*, reserved for God and *veneration* for Mary and the saints.

The grammar in grammar school. One day in sixth grade my teacher, Sister Mary Celestine, a fat, pleasant woman asked,

"What is correct: *It was she,* or *It was her.*"

Silence from the scholars seated before her.

I raised my hand. She said, "Pat."

I said, "It was she."

"Why?"

"Because *was* is a linking verb and it takes a nominative complement."

"And?"

"*Her* is objective case. *She* is nominative."

She smiled pleasantly and I thought, "I totally love this shit!"

My friend Tom Murphy who was sitting across the aisle from me might have thought I was speaking in tongues.

In seventh grade I had Sister Catherine Ann, a very young woman—slim and with a very pretty face which was all you could see with her habit and veil. She taught religion, reading, social studies, science, and arithmetic in the morning (9 a.m. to 12 p.m.). In the afternoon, she taught spelling for about 20 minutes and grammar for the rest of the afternoon (1:20 p.m. to 3 p.m.). We diagramed sentences. We talked about the *subjunctive mood* and the *progressive aspect* of verbs. It is quite possible that Sister Catherine Ann and I were the only people in the room who were having a good time.

Liking academics and knowing what teachers know. When I was in seventh grade. I liked understanding the subjunctive mood and the progressive aspect of verbs for the same reason that I liked knowing the parts of a cathedral. I admired my teachers and they knew these things and that was enough for me.

In 1961 when I was teaching English in a public high school, I ventured into a little discussion of English grammar — a thing that would have been frowned upon by the school administration as not being "progressive." Only one girl in the class seemed to know what I was talking about. I asked her if she had gone to a Catholic elementary school, and she answered yes. Another girl in the class became incensed: "Why were they learning stuff in Catholic school that kids in public school weren't learning?" Good question.

When most people talk about grammar, they are really referring to usage — Don't say, "*Ain't.*" *Ain't* has nothing to do with grammar. It's simply nonstandard usage. Standard English usage is the usage of educated, affluent, powerful speakers of English in fairly formal settings. Standard English usage was originally the usage of the London upper crust — London, the seat of government, commerce and, the church. If you were a country bumpkin your English usage gave you away. If you wanted to get on in London, you learned to talk like an upper crust Londoner. It was not "good grammar." It was the usage of high-status individuals — the newscasters on NBC for example.

By the time I got to graduate school William Labov had demonstrated that every language in use has its own grammar, and so, no language is "ungrammatical." Labov demonstrated this by recording the English language of Black people in a part of New York City and writing its grammar. It was "good grammar" because it accurately described the language of a particular group of people. Therefore, the language of high social class people is no more or less "grammatical" than the language of people of lower social class. It's all about the status of the language *users*, not the "correctness" of their language.

And that for me opened a door. The study of the interaction between language and social class has profound social, political, and economic consequences. My interest in studying this topic dominated my career and has helped me explain myself to myself years later when I began writing this memoir, and I believe it all began when I raised my hand in Sister Mary Celestine's 6th grade classroom and said, "It was *she,* because *was* is a linking verb and it takes a nominative complement."

Grammar is rarely taught in grades 1 through 12 these days. When it is taught, it is likely to be in schools with a fairly affluent student body, and it is not taught to improve students' spoken and written English usage. Students from affluent homes are taught to understand and manipulate systems rather than to simply learn facts, and so grammar is taught as a *system* that can be understood.

I taught grammar for 50 years in middle school, high school, college, and graduate school. I have a master's degree in American Linguistics and Literature, and a Ph.D. in Education from the University of Chicago. While on the faculty of the Graduate School of Education at the University at Buffalo, I taught students preparing to become English teachers.

Over these many years there have been many iterations of the way English grammar is conceived— Structural Linguistics, Transformational Grammar, Case Grammar (a flash in the pan, but the basis of my Ph.D. dissertation), Psycholinguistics, and Sociolinguistics. My most successful book, *Literacy with an Attitude: Educating Working-Class Children in Their Own Self-Interest*, grew out of my interest in ethnography—the study of social class and language. I understood all of these instantly, and always through the lens of the traditional school grammar that I learned in seventh grade.

When I published my first book, *Helping Children Learn to Read*, in 1985, I wrote to Sister Catherine Ann at the Mother House of the Sisters of Providence in St. Mary of the Woods, Indiana, and I told her how I shared her interest in grammar and how it had facilitated my understanding of language for my entire academic career. She answered me saying congratulations on the book; she thought she remembered me; and she was no longer teaching. She occupied herself with prayer and adoration of the Blessed Sacrament. A lovely woman who led an admirable life. Eight years of daily contact with such women was a very good thing.

I liked knowing that linking verbs took nominative complements. I admired my teachers and I liked knowing what they knew.

The library on 79th Street. If you asked me from the time I was in sixth grade until I was at least fifty who my best friend was, I'd say Tommy Murphy. He was in the same grade at St. Leo Grammar School and we were in the same classroom in grades five through eight. He lived less than a block from me — down the alley, across 78th Street and a few houses further down the alley.

Murphy's father was an office manager in a downtown firm of some kind. He was the only person I knew who took the Rock Island to and from work. I remember being in Murphy's backyard when he came through the gate dressed in a suit with a white shirt and tie and with the evening *Chicago Times* under his arm. Murphy's parents had more middle-class ideas about child rearing than my parents. They had only three children — Tommy and an older brother and sister, Billy and Geraldine.

Mrs. Murphy took Tommy and me to "story hour" at the public library one summer day when I was about ten. The library was only about two blocks from both our houses. I never went to story hour again, but I knew where the library was, and I had been inside it, and I liked being there. I got a library card and I began going there fairly often. I doubt Murphy ever darkened the library door again.

The library was on 79th Street, a streetcar line. It was probably four storefronts wide. There were circulation counters parallel to the sidewalls as you entered — the children and "junior" counter on the left and the adult counter on the right. The left half of the library was divided into two sections — the children's books near the front and the junior books further back. The adult section took up the entire right half of the floor. The rooms were furnished with heavy oak tables and chairs — appropriate-sized for little kids, bigger kids, and adults. It was quiet, alien, and strange, but pleasant and "gilded by the promise of sophistication."

My cousin Georgine was an assistant librarian at the 79th Street library, a job she probably got through Finn family clout, and so a chat with her (in whispers, of course) was part of a visit to the library. I probably took home and read a dozen books about two boy detectives named Tom Playfair and Percy Winn. They were like the Hardy Boys, but the author, Francis J. Finn, was a Jesuit priest who wrote under the name "Father Finn." I probably chose the Tom Playfair series over the Hardy Boys because the author was a priest named Finn.

When I was in seventh grade, we were assigned to

write a research paper. We were given a list of possible topics and I chose "scorpions." I went to the library as instructed and the librarian showed me the encyclopedia shelf and explained how to look things up. I probably copied a few paragraphs and handed it in. I don't think Sister Catharine Ann expected me to do anything more. But I think it took hours and when I was finished, I knew that you could find out almost anything if you had a topic and understood alphabetical order. I liked knowing that.

In high school I was introduced to a little more serious literature and I fell under the spell of Sinclair Lewis's *Arrowsmith,* and Dickens's *A Tale of Two Cities* in a way that I was never to experience again in reading. I reread *A Tale of Two Cities* many years later and was very surprised at how sappy it seemed to me as an adult.

Today I attend the symphony two or three times a year, "Live from The Met" occasionally, and a Shakespeare play about once a year. It still seems a little like homework, but I persist in thinking homework is the right thing to do, and I do enjoy them in the end. I do not, however, appreciate much of 20th century symphonic music. It's too hard, and my neurosis simply cannot keep up.

As I began to like knowing about schoolish things and to appreciate classical music, literature, and theater, I was somewhat aware that this was setting me apart from my working-class family and community, and not in a good way. But, like my being uninterested in sports, I didn't care. Most people around me did not notice, particularly my mother who really did not pay a lot of attention to me. But Norrine noticed and she encouraged me. It became our sophistication project.

The taste of an olive. In the 1944 blockbuster movie "Going My Way," Bing Crosby starred as a young Catholic priest who is newly assigned to a White working-class parish in New York City. He turns a bunch of teen-aged boys into a church choir that looks like "The Dead-end Kids." In fact, they were The Dead-end Kids— juvenile actors Leo Gorcey, Huntz Hall, William Benedict, and others who were featured in a series of 1940s movies such as "The Dead-End Kids," "The Bowery Boys," and the "East Side Kids."

In "Going My Way," as Bing's unlikely church choir, they sing backup for his rendition of "Swinging on a Star." This takes place during choir practice. In another story line in the movie Bing sings "Tura Lura Lura" in a scene where the aged parishpastor (Barry Fitzgerald) is reunited on his deathbed with his even more aged mother whom Bing has secretly brought over from Ireland. In 1944, this was flat out Catholic rapture.

In the midst of all this schmaltz, there is a scene where Rise Stevens sings the "Habanera" from *Carmen* on the stage of the New York Metropolitan Opera as Bing Crosby watches from the wings. (It seems that the priest and the opera star were sweethearts before he entered the priesthood.) This was somewhat typical fare for movies in the 40s and 50s. In an effort to bring culture to the masses, a scene from an opera, ballet, or a snippet from a symphony concert was often worked into popular movies, especially musicals.

I don't know if at nine years of age I actually liked listening to Rise Stevens singing "Habanera," but I am sure I thought I was supposed to like it. The feeling was aptly described in a book review I once read where the reviewer comments on a character in a novel's first experience of classical music:"It was like the first time he had tasted an olive. It was unlike anything that had crossed his palate before; strange and not quite pleasant, yet gilded by the promise of sophistication."

I am certain I did not know what *sophistication* meant when I was nine, but I knew that that unnamed thing was something I wanted to have. And because I've always had a tendency to be neurotic, to accept that sophistication is a thing I *should* acquire and to fail to achieve it would have made me feel guilty. By the way, I love olives, but I remember that my first taste was "strange and not quite pleasant, yet gilded by the promise of sophistication."

Only a year after "Going My Way," in the 1945 Hollywood biopic, "A Song to Remember," Coronel Wilde plays Frederick Chopin and Merle Oberon plays George Sand. Oberon was Anglo-Indian (born in Mumbai) which accounted for her stunning and exotic beauty. In "A Song to Remember" Chopin's piano concertos are played triumphantly in the most dramatic scenes. At age 10, I didn't *think* I should like it; I *knew* I loved it.

I was well aware that working-class Irish boys on the Southside of Chicago in 1945 were supposed to find Bizet's "Habanera" and Chopin's "Polonaise" non-starters, if not repellent. I just didn't care. As I grew older my taste in music never became all that sophisticated. A former boss who was a very serious music lover described my taste in music as "Beethoven with all the stops out."

When I was in eighth grade at St. Leo Grammar School they marched my class over to St. Leo High School one afternoon to see a student production of "Seven Keys to Baldpate," a Broadway play written by George M. Cohan 30 years earlier. By 1949 it had become standard amateur theater fare. It was the first time I had ever seen actors on a stage. I was captivated, and I have loved legitimate theater ever since.

When I was in high school (on days I actually went to school) I would spend study periods in the library reading plays in a series of books called *The Best Plays of 1945, The Best Plays of 1946,* and so on. During my college days I was into Sartre and existentialism and I think I read every Eugene O'Neill play. Brooding seemed like the right thing for an aspiring young Irish "intellectual" to do. Looking back, I realize that it was also was part of my sophistication project.

Brud noticed my liking academics and the arts, and he worried about me. He dropped by on Union Avenue one Sunday afternoon while I was in high school, and I was watching "Omnibus" — a Sunday afternoon program that showcased classical music, ballet, modern dance, and theater. It was disparagingly referred to as "the culture ghetto." The Ford Foundation in fact, sponsored it in an effort to "raise the level of American taste." Brud said imploringly, "Why do you watch that stuff?" He was concerned that as a working-class man, interest in that kind of stuff would bring me nothing but grief. I always knew Brud loved me and his disapproval was genuinely out of concern. But by this time, I just didn't care whether I fit in.

Chapter 9.

TROUBLING EVENTS

In a 1947 blockbuster biopic "The Jolson Story," Larry Parks plays Al Jolson, the star of the first talking picture. Jolson was the best known and highest paid performer in America in the 1930s. His most famous act featured him standing alone on a dark stage in a solitary spotlight wearing a tuxedo, white gloves, and minstrel-show blackface makeup and singing songs such as "Sewanee," "April Showers," "Sonny Boy", Rock-A-Boy Baby With A Dixie Melody," and, most famously, "My Mammy."

"My Mammy." Because St. Leo Grammar School had no playground, they would close off the street in front of the church, rectory, clubhouse, and school buildings with traffic horses, and the barricaded street and sidewalk became our playground during lunch hour and for about 30 minutes before school started at 9:00 a.m. One of the happiest episodes of my life occurred when I was in sixth grade before school started one morning on that "playground."

Tommy Murphy and I were imitating Jolson singing "My Mammy" on the steps of the church with probably 20 of our classmates surrounding us and egging us on. There were about one hundred students in each of the eight grades at St. Leo Grammar School and I counted every kid in my grade as a friend. I was popular. I was known for my sense of humor. I got good grades. Life was good.

Troubling events. But between sixth and ninth grades events occurred that set me up for what were undoubtedly the most troubled years of my life — my high school years: Norrine's marriage and subsequent divorce; my father's death; and going to Calumet High School, probably as the result of my father's death, rather than St. Leo High School or one of the other Catholic Boys high schools on the Southside of Chicago, as did nearly every other boy in my grammar school graduation class.

There was also the plight of Black people fleeing into northern cities from the Jim Crow South, especially as lynchings intensified. During and after World War II it became known as the Second Great Migration (the First Great Migration happened during and after World War I.) This Second Great Migration created the greatest social, political, economic, moral, and spiritual challenges of my lifetime, and the Catholic Church in Chicago — where I had felt so safe and so certain — failed miserably to meet the challenge with moral or spiritual guidance.

I was just nine and Norrine was twenty-two when World War II ended in the summer of 1945. The dating scene was, of course, very lively as marriageable neighborhood boys who had been away for as long as four years began returning home. Sometime that fall Norrine met a young veteran at The Three Pats, which, among the taverns on Halsted Street, was the one the younger set frequented. His name was Bob Kearney. He was handsome and charming and he and Norrine were married the following year.

They had their first child, Maryann, a year later. Soon after they were married, it was apparent that he had a serious alcohol problem, exacerbated, no doubt, by what would be called "post-traumatic stress syndrome" today. He had had a harrowing war experience. He was in and out of the Hines Veterans Administration Hospital in Maywood, a Chicago suburb, for the next several years.

Norrine moved back into Union Avenue with Maryann and went back to work at a ceramic factory to support herself and her baby. For the next few years Norrine tried to keep her marriage together. She spent weekends with Kearney while he was on passes from the veteran's hospital, and she had a second child, Danny. At some point it became apparent that Kearney could not or would not help himself, and Norrine gave up and they were divorced — a near catastrophe in our close-knit Irish Catholic neighborhood.

Soon after her divorce, Norrine got a job as a night operator (midnight to 8 a.m.) at NuPhone, a telephone answering service above Walgreens at 79th and Halsted, and Maryann and Danny went to nursery school and later elementary school at St. Leo. My mother got the kids off to school. Norrine slept while they were at school and was up to take care of them when they got home. I filled in a lot as a babysitter.

When Maryann was about seven and Danny about five, Norrine married Willie Janecek. Willie adopted Maryann and Danny and they moved into a house in Berwyn, a suburb of Chicago. Then she and Willie had three children: Little William, who died a few months after he was born with an inoperable congenital heart defect, Judeanne, and Mike. Norrine and Willie remained married until Willie's death more than 50 years later. Norrine lived to be 91.

Daddy's death. On February 1, 1948, my father, age 50, died of a sudden heart attack, in the midst of these post war events. I remember the night very vividly. It was a Saturday night. My mother and father had gone next door to a graduation party for the neighbor's oldest son, Leo. In those days there were two graduation days in the Chicago school system, one at the end of each semester in January and June. Leo had graduated at the end of January.

I had gone to bed around ten, but I was awakened around midnight when Jack, Joan, and my cousins Patsy and Georgine came in the front door rather noisily. I heard their conversation as they entered the house and it aroused my interest. I spent around a half hour leaning over the banister of the front hall stairs listening to their conversation from the kitchen. Patsy was telling them about a wild party in her kitchen where friends of her parents got into an argument, and the wife picked up a Canada Dry Ginger Ale quart bottle and hit her husband on the side of the head with it. Soda came in heavy glass bottles in those days. The bottle was empty, but she still might have killed him. Luckily, she did not.

I lost interest after a while when the conversation changed to more mundane matters and went back to bed. About 1:00 a.m. my parents came home, Patsy and Georgine left, and everyone went to bed. Jim, the oldest of us not yet married, came home from a date about an hour later, but I did not hear him. Around 4 a.m. I heard my mother banging on the bathroom door and shouting, "Dan! Dan!" and then, "Jimmy, Daddy fell in the bathroom, and he won't answer me!"

Jimmy came running from his bedroom and down the hall and forced the bathroom door open and yelled, "Don't come in here, Ma!" which of course she did. My father was lying on the bathroom floor and not breathing. Whether he got out of bed because he felt ill, or was having chest pains, or just had to pee, we will never know. But he had gotten up, gone into the bathroom, locked the door, and fell on the floor with enough force for my mother to hear him falling from their bedroom. Someone—Jimmy? Mary? The whole house was up by this time—ran downstairs to the phone and called the fire department.

Mickey and I shared a double bed in the front bedroom at the time. We were ordered to stay in bed and were assured that Daddy had fallen, but the fire department was coming and he would be all right. When the fire department arrived, seemingly in a matter of minutes, they had with them what was called a Pulmotor—an early version of what was later called a Resuscitator. It is a mask attached to an oxygen tank. They put the mask over the mouth and nose of a patient who had stopped breathing and forced air into their his or her lungs.

From our bedroom where Mickey and I were sitting up in the bed cross-legged by this time, I could hear the air being pumped and released for perhaps five minutes. When it stopped, I thought he was all right, but my mother began to really wail, as did my older brothers and sisters who were in the hall. My father was dead of a heart attack. He had probably died as soon as he entered the bathroom, perhaps even before his body hit the floor. I am quite certain that I did not cry. I sensed the profound import of what had happened, but I did not feel grief. Up until the moment after the Pulmotor stopped, I thought he would be all right.

I had been in the habit of regaling Tommy Murphy and sometimes other friends with family stories, like the day Bob thought Jack had drowned in the bathtub. I suppose such stories exist in many families, but with a family of eleven pretty boisterous individuals, stories like this abound. And so, I sat there cross-legged in the middle of the bed, listening to the hiss of the Pulmotor and confident that my father would be O.K., I was actually composing the story in my head of all the comings and goings of this night, thinking that this is going to be one hell of a story.

Somehow, even after the Pulmotor stopped, and it was clear that my father was dead, I might have wailed, because everyone else was wailing, but I did not feel grief. I felt I should feel grief, and I tried to feel grief, but I did not feel grief. I blamed my father for what I perceived to be my mother's unhappiness, and I was not sorry he was gone.

My father was waked at Sheehy's Funeral Home for three nights before his funeral. Over a hundred people came each night to pay their respects which speaks to my father's reputation and influence in union circles and to his active participation in organizations such as the Veterans of Foreign Wars, The American Legion, The Ancient Order of Hibernians, The Holy Name Society, and a half-dozen others. I spent these four days trying to convince myself that I loved my father and I would miss him, but I could not convince myself.

Despite the happy times I had witnessed between my parents when they were making Sunday dinner or the times they were working together on a decorating project, my abiding impression of their relationship was that they were unhappy with one another. They argued angrily from opposite ends of the table nearly every night while the nine of us sat and listened. I felt certain that they truly hated each other. I pitied her and I blamed him.

My sister Joan, who is four years older than I, told me many years later that the bone of contention at the dinner table was my brother Jack, who was sickly, and my father thought my mother babied him. Joan blamed my mother and felt sorry for my father. She told me in this same conversation that my father had a special affection for me. He called me his "Guardian Angel." I wish he had lived long enough for me to know him when I was an adult. I later learned that there was much about him that was admirable.

Chapter 10.

CALUMET HIGH SCHOOL

As every other boy in my eighth-grade class was discussing whether he would be going to St. Leo High School or one of the other Catholic boy's high schools on Chicago's Southside, it became clear that I would not going to St. Leo High School. I would be going to Calumet, the public high school. That was probably due to the changes in our family finances after my father's death, but it was never discussed or explained.

I would no longer be cutting through Clancy's back yard to the tender ministrations of the Sisters of Providence at St. Leo Grammar School with its largely Irish working-class student body, and dozens of friends whom I had known since first grade. Instead, I would be walking alone a mile southwest of 78th and Union to Calumet, to an enormous public high school and the tutelage of very good lay teachers.

The first hour of my first day at Calumet, a teacher asked a boy a question and he answered, "Ya." I waited for the roof to fall in. At St. Leo Grammar School you answered, "Yes, Sister" when a nun asked you a question. Answering, "Ya," would have been seen as the height of insolence. The teacher did not seem to notice and I decided, "This is a place I do not belong, and where I do not want to be. Someone get me out of here." No one was listening.

I tried and succeeded in making myself invisible at Calumet for the next four years. I was never bullied; I was just ignored. I had only two friends, Donald Hansen and Robert Lee. They too were probably outcasts. I ate lunch with them but never saw them at any other time. I don't think they saw one another except at lunch either.

Robert was Jewish and one day during our junior year while we were walking on campus during the lunch hour he said something like, "I've had enough of that already." I recognized this use of *already* as a Jewish turn of phrase, and I said to Robert that he should not say *already* as much as he did. He asked why, and I just said, "I don't know. It just sounds funny." I think we both knew that I meant, "It sounds like something a Jew would say." The implication was that he *naturally* would not want to remind people he was Jewish.

We did not pursue the matter, but one day at lunch I said something that really offended him. It probably was something anti-Semitic, but intended to be funny. He picked up his tray and moved to another table. We never spoke again. In fact, I don't remember ever seeing him again. Many years later, after the inception of the Internet, I tried unsuccessfully to find Robert Lee. I did really like him and I was sorry I did not try harder to explain and apologize.

Enrolling in college prep. The Calumet High School district was geographically very large and it included both working-class neighborhoods like the one surrounding St. Leo church and middle-class neighborhoods like the one surrounding the high school. Based largely on entrance exams, student behavior, and parent interventions, students at Calumet were sorted into two cohorts referred to as "college preparatory" and "regular." For well-documented reasons, middle-class students tended to be assigned to the college preparatory group and working-class students tended to be assigned to the regular group, and as a result there were two schools in the same building, one working-class and one middle-class.

When I registered at Calumet I scored very well on the entrance exams, and I probably checked "College Preparatory Curriculum" on my registration forms. I had no reason to expect that I would be going to college when I started high school. I suppose it was just part of Norrine's and my sophistication project, but I was placed in the college prep program, and so my experience at Calumet was one of a student in a very good middle-class public high school.

The college preparatory curriculum consisted of high-status knowledge—algebra, geometry and calculus rather than business arithmetic—*Macbeth* and *A Tale of Two Cities* rather than *The Red Badge of Courage*. The French philosopher Pierre Bourdieu referred to this as "cultural capital" because with it you can buy middle-class status which in turn buys real capital—that is wealth.

In my first semester at Calumet, I took Latin, Algebra, English, World History, General Science, and Music appreciation. I received all S's [Superior] and E's, [Excellent] grades in all my classes. I was on the Honor Roll, and had near perfect attendance, but for the remaining seven semesters I received only F's [Fair], barely passing – in every subject, semester after semester, and I was absent at least one day every week.

My attendance. The rule was that if a student were absent more than 20 days (on average one day a week in a 20-week semester), they had to take and pass tests in every subject. These tests were administered in the school lunchroom on a specified day. The reason they were given was probably to satisfy some state requirement that students with excessive absences show basic mastery of course work to receive credit. On the day the tests were administered around 100 students showed up in the lunchroom and there might have been two monitors.

There was nearly as much talking as there was during a lunch period except that everyone was whispering – that is cheating. The tests were very easy. I usually passed the tests easily but my second semester Latin test asked for the conjugation of a particular verb. I didn't have a clue. Luckily, ahem, my Latin textbook was at my elbow. I opened it and the conjugation *of that verb* was easily available. I had no worries about getting caught. No one was trying to catch anyone. I doubt that anyone ever read those tests.

I never "ditched" school, that is I never left the house but did not go to school. I just announced that I wasn't going to school and my mother would register a little displeasure but say, "O.K." She would write the same note every time: "Patrick missed school yesterday because he was needed at home." Miss McEnroe, my freshman algebra teacher, supervised a study hall I was in during my junior year. She would call me to her desk and chat.

She was the only teacher who ever mentioned my absences, but in the same breath she would comment understandingly that I was "needed at home." She no doubt imagined that I was the oldest of seven children of a widowed mother who worked as a temporary day laborer one day a week to keep food on the table. Neither she nor anyone else ever asked why I was needed at home so much.

I was never moved out of the College Preparatory stream. I was clearly capable of doing the work. I was one of those students—I've had dozens of them in my teaching career—who were no trouble, who passed tests when they happened to be in class to take tests, but who were frequently absent, and rarely handed in homework. You just give them a passing grade and call it a day.

Neither Norrine nor my mother took any notice that my school attendance and grades plunged after my first semester of high school. Norrine's struggle to keep her own life together during this time took all the energy she had, and my mother was still in her "No trouble from you, no attention from me" mode. Fair enough, my father died two years earlier and she had five children still in school.

Delivery boy. There was a reason why my grades and school attendance plummeted after my first semester at Calumet. Near the end of that semester, a telephone call came to our house from Mrs. Tarr, the wife of Frank Tarr, a butcher who owned a shop at 78th and Halsted Street. They needed a new delivery boy, and Mrs. Tarr said the Finns had been recommended because we were a "good family" and had a bunch of boys. I was dispatched, and I got the job.

I delivered meat on a bicycle with an extra-large basket every day after school from 3:30 till 6:00 p. m. and on Saturdays from 9:00 a. m. to 6:00 p.m. — rain, snow, or shine, ten degrees or ninety degrees. At 6:00 p.m., on Monday through Thursday, Mr. Tarr (I always addressed him simply as "Tarr") would empty the cash register, put the cash into a pouch, put the pouch into his pocket, tuck a revolver into his waist band, put on his coat or jacket, and walk home about three blocks away. I never knew whether Tarr had a gun permit, nor did I wonder. That he carried a gun did not seem remarkable to me. I don't remember where he kept the gun in the shop, and I don't think I knew. Being held up was unheard of in our neighborhood.

When Tarr left for home, I stayed on to scrape the butcher's blocks with a steel brush, clean the lunch-meat slicer, clean the glass on the front of the meat counter, "rake" the floor (covered with sawdust as was the custom in butcher shops), generally straighten up, and lock up. I frequently sliced myself a bit of ham and had a few cookies from the bulk containers. This no doubt exacerbated my weight problem. (I was very skinny til sixth grade when I became decidedly not.)

And so, on Monday through Wednesday, I'd finish about 6:30 p. m., but on Thursday through Saturday I had additional chores. Every week Tarr would produce signs that announced the week's sales on 24" by 36" butchers' wrapping paper with a paintbrush and red and blue tempera paint.

CENTER CUT PORK CHOPS

39¢

HOME MADE PORK SAUSAGE

29¢

On Thursdays, in addition to deliveries, I would take down the previous week's sale signs from inside the shop window, wash the window inside and out with soapy water and a brush and squeegee, and hang the new signs for the coming week. I also made pork sausage on Thursdays.

Tarr kept a separate pail next to his block for pork fat that he trimmed from roasts and chops. On Thursdays he would add enough lean pork to make pork sausage, and I would grind it up with the meat grinder in the walk-in refrigerator. Tarr would add the proper spices to the ground meat, and I would mix it together with well-scrubbed bare hands to evenly distribute the meat and fat and spices. Earlier, Tarr would have taken a supply of pork small intestines kept

111

in salt in the walk-in cooler and put them in a pan full of water to make them supple.

Using a contraption that looked like a giant version of the tool you use to decorate a cake with icing, I would load the barrel with ground sausage meat, and, turning a handle, force the sausage meat into a nozzle and into the pork gut — creating a long continuous sausage link about two inches in diameter. I'd form these sausage lengths into a coil and place them on a display tray in the meat counter. Then, of course, I washed the sausage-making contraption. And so, on Thursdays I worked until 7:00 or 7:30.

On Fridays I dressed chickens after making deliveries and before cleaning up. Chickens were delivered to the shop sans feathers, heads, and feet, but the innards needed to be removed, the gizzards separated from the intestines, and the liver separated from the gall bladder. The hearts, gizzards, and livers were returned to the cavity for the customer to use in cooking or throw away. If the customer wanted the chicken cut up, I removed the legs and wings, separated the drumsticks from the thighs, removed the breast portion from the back, and split the breast in two, using a sharp knife.

I was absent-minded then as I have always been, particularly while doing routine tasks, and occasionally I cut up a roasting chicken that was supposed to be left whole. This would make Tarr really angry, but mostly he liked me. Mrs. Tarr told me that he was really fond of me and I believed her. Fridays I worked until about 9 p.m. On Saturdays I delivered groceries from 9 till 6 and did my usual clean up except that I'd sweep up the sawdust and put fresh sawdust down on the floors. There was a lot of end-of-the-week special cleaning of trays, counters, and so on, and so we had extra help. For a while that was my younger brother, Mickey.

What I missed most while I was working at Tarr's, were the happy, noisy, Saturday mornings in the kitchen on Union Avenue. Those of us who were still living at home, woke up for the day, straggled downstairs and into the kitchen, poured coffee, and sat down at the table. (I do not remember a time when I did not drink coffee.) Married siblings came in with some of their kids and joined the gathering. There was a lot of loud talking and laughing and horsing around.

One of these mornings, my sister Mary, who has a beautiful soprano voice, got up to leave the kitchen to get dressed for the day. As she left the kitchen, she burst into a somewhat abridged version of a song that was popular at the time. The actual words were, "Roll or bowl the ball, a penny a pitch!" Mary's full-throated version rendered for no apparent reason was "Roll or bowl the ball, you son of a bitch!"

When I had deliveries that took me near our house I would stop in, grab a cup of coffee, join the fun, and then get back on my bike and return to the shop, hoping that Mrs. Tarr, who acted as a telephone order taker, cashier, and a sort of manager of the shop, had not noticed that I was gone for a little too long. I don't recall that she ever did.

And so, I was working over 30 hours a week for $15 plus tips for deliveries—probably another $5. Tips were generally ten or twenty cents; twenty-five cent tips were rare. I gave my mother $10 for "board" leaving me with about $10, a lot of money for a teenager in 1950. Bob "borrowed" around $5 every Saturday night. He would convince me that he was going out, and I probably was not. There always seemed to be some sort of logic in that. He was probably still trading on the affection and admiration I felt for him when we were younger. He never paid me back. Neither of us ever really thought he would.

Chapter 11.

WAYS WITH WORDS

At St. Leo Grammar School, the religion, English, reading, history, geography, and even arithmetic textbooks were all especially written for Catholic schools—Scott Foresman's "Cathedral Editions." Arithmetic was learning rules. Reading consisted of word recognition, vocabulary building, and literal comprehension of meaning. History was memorizing dates. Events in history were examined in strict accordance with church doctrine. There was rarely any discussion and if there were, it took the form of students contributing facts or opinions that everyone agreed upon.

In my classes at Calumet, textbooks were less parochial, and teachers encouraged discussion. And since there was a more diverse student body, students offered conflicting opinions and disputed facts offered by others. A student responding to a teacher's question with, "Ya," was part of a collegiality between teachers and students that would have been seen as insolence at St. Leo Grammar School.

All this gave rise to academic discourse— the language of the academy— and I felt very much at home with it. In fact, while I didn't converse with other students much, I talked a lot in class discussions. And as I became more and more at home in these high school classes, I found myself unwittingly becoming more and more alienated from my working-class Irish Catholic home and community.

In her wonderful book, *Ways with Words,* ethnographer Shirley Brice Heath studied the social arrangements and language behavior of two communities located within a mile of each other — one working-class and one middle-class. She described her working-class community as a "society of intimates" and her middle-class community as a "society of strangers." She might as well have been describing the working-class world of the Finn Family versus the middle-class world that I was introduced to at Calumet High School.

The Irish Catholic working-class community that I grew up in was indeed a society of intimates. Gender roles, parent-child roles, sibling roles, and the roles of those in authority (police, priests, teachers, adults in general) were fairly rigidly understood and accepted. Everyone knew how to act, how to talk, and, quite often, what to say.

A woman from one such community put it something like this: *You do right, and you say right, and you're right, and everyone knows you're right. You do wrong, or you say wrong, and you're wrong, and everyone knows you're wrong; and if you don't accept that, you just don't fit in.* As a result of this intimacy, meanings, feelings, and beliefs tend to be implied rather than stated explicitly.

The middle-class community I found myself immersed in at Calumet was a society of strangers. It is not that people in such communities do not know one another or that they do not have close relationships with one another. It is just that they do not assume to know what others in their community know or what others believe regarding many topics. That has an effect on how they talk to one another. They tend to state meanings and opinions explicitly and differences of opinion, discussion, argument, and individuality are encouraged.

A British ethnographer observed that working-class people tend to find middle-class people's language tiresome, if not laughable, because middle-class people tend to state facts explicitly that everyone present already knows and to state opinions explicitly that everyone shares. It is no accident that there is so much overlap between academic discourse and the language of a society of strangers. They are both the language of middle-class communities.

Despite my poor grades, some of my teachers took note of my aptitude for schoolwork. Miss McEnroe, my algebra teacher, told me I had a gift for math, "mathematical intuition" she called it. She encouraged me to enter a mathematics department competition. The top student would get an award from the math department. I didn't enter because the competition would be held on a Saturday and by second semester, I was working every Saturday.

When I was in 10th grade Tom Murphy and I went downtown to the "Railroad Fair" on Chicago's lakefront one

Sunday afternoon. This was a sort of an outdoor museum dedicated to the history of the railroad and a celebration of Chicago's central role in it. It was the first time I took a streetcar downtown without an adult. Murphy and I either got lost or we were just wandering around, but we passed an enormous downtown Catholic Church and went in to see inside. A little further along we found ourselves in Chicago's Skid Row, with its vagrants and squalor.

The following week I wrote a "theme" for my English class about this adventure comparing the atmosphere of the church to that of Skid Row. Miss Satler, my English teacher who introduced herself to the class by saying she was one "t" short of being a hotel heiress (Satler/Statler — get it?), read my theme to the class and gave it an "E+," not an "S", or even an "S- because I had spelled *stopped* — s-t-o-p-e-d. I was one "*p*" short of getting an "S."

Miss Sabatus, my 11th grade English teacher, also recognized my aptitude for writing — albeit in a negative way. I handed in a theme to her that I had written 30 minutes earlier in a study hall. This was during the Korean War, and my paper was on the military draft. She returned the papers the following week, but she did not return mine. She asked me to stay after class, which I did. My paper in hand, she said, "Where did you copy this from?" I was shocked. "I didn't copy it," I said. "I wrote it in 6th period study hall." "You did not write this paper, Pat," she said. "I should bring you to the principal's office, but I'm going to ask you to write another paper and don't try anything like this again."

I didn't persist in denying it. I just said, "O.K." and I wrote another paper. It's not like any of this mattered to me at the time. I was going to get an "F" on that course the way I did in every course for my last seven semesters at Calumet. In my forty years of teaching students from grade 5 through Ph.D. students in graduate school, I have suspected at times that students have handed me a plagiarized or partly plagiarized paper. The evidence had to be really overwhelming before I ever made anything of it.

While teaching at a Chicago Community College, I actually went to the library and found the only book on the topic that a student had written his paper on. I found that he had copied the preface of the book word for word. In the face of this evidence, he denied it. I said, "I should report this to the dean's office, but I won't. Write another paper and if it's satisfactory I'll give it a 'C.'" *Deja vu!*

As little as I attended school, I did enough of the reading and I did enough of the assignments to avoid flat-out failing, and I soaked up every teacher's word when I was in class. Nothing else in the classroom, like other students — particularly other students — distracted me.

I can still see Mr. Sietsema, my geometry teacher, hopping across the front of the room as if on rocks in a stream (known facts) from one "shore" (the problem) to the far shore (the solution). This was the deductive method. He then hopped backwards from rock to rock from the far shore to the near shore. This was the inductive method.

And seventy years later I can still hear Miss Stellar, my third-year English teacher, reading Emily Dickinson's "The Railway Train."

> *I like to see it lap the miles,*
> *And lick the valleys up,*
> *And stop to feed itself at tanks;*
> *And then, prodigious, step*
> *Around a pile of mountains,*
> *....*
> *Then, punctual as a star,*
> *Stop — docile and omnipotent —*
> *At its own stable door.*

And I can hear Miss Stellar reading the following lines from Macbeth,

> *Macbeth: If we should fail?*
> *Lady Macbeth: We Fail.*

and asking *as if it really mattered*, "Did Shakespeare intend for Lady Macbeth to mean 'Well, at least we tried.' Or did he intend for her words to mean, 'Are you kidding? How can we fail?'" Miss Stellar's recitation of Dickenson and her passionate interest in what those two words from Shakespeare were meant to convey was mesmerizing.

All of this was heightened by the fact that Miss Stellar was probably about 50, but had a girlish figure, and sometimes wore blouses with necklines low enough to expose just a little cleavage. She had straight black hair combed straight back off her face, and she wore a lot of red rouge. According to student lore she was an American Indian. I was mad about her. Mr. Seitsema's geometry lectures and Miss Stellar's dramatic readings of literature were once again unlike anything I had experienced before: strange and gilded by the promise of sophistication—like the guy with the olive.

This was the cultural and academic capital that I would not have acquired had I not been in the college preparation curriculum and had the learning experience of a typical middle-class student in a really good middle-class school. But this did not happen without my paying a price. As I began to talk and act and be interested in things that made me welcome in an academic discourse community, these same behaviors were alienating me from the working-class home, parish, and community. It took me years of study in sociology, linguistics and ethnography to understand all this, but I am certain that if I had understood it at the time, I would have followed the same path that I chose then.

Chapter 12.

ETHNIC STRIFE, RACIAL STRIFE and EUGENICS

Northern troops occupied the former Confederate states from 1865 to 1877, the period known as Reconstruction. During that time former slaves made some progress toward economic security and full citizenship. Black people were even elected to state and federal offices. But when Union troops were withdrawn from the former Confederate states in 1877 there commenced what became known as "Jim Crow" governance.

It was named after "Jim Crow," a stock character in the "minstrel shows" that had become popular throughout the country in the decades before the Civil War. White men in blackface sang and danced and generally mimicked Black people, holding them up to ridicule and portraying them as happy with their lives on the plantation.

On Halloween a lot of kids in my neighborhood, including me, wore blackface for "Trick or Treating." Corks came in a lot of bottles in those days. You could simply hold a cork in the gas-stove flame for a few seconds. The cork would start to burn; you would let it burn for a few seconds and blow it out. It cooled off immediately and you rubbed the burnt cork onto your face. Photographs of prominent White politicians in blackface have surfaced well into the present century and they were explained away as harmless, college boys' folly.

Minstrels were popular fundraising events in White churches and social organizations well into the 1960s. When I was in seventh grade, St. Leo parish put on a minstrel show in the grammar school auditorium, and my mother, who had a beautiful singing voice, sang "Mammy," an Al Jolson favorite. She appeared alone in a spotlight, stage right, on the darkened stage, wearing an Aunt Jemima costume (white kerchief around her head, a floor length red and white checkered dress and white apron) — and, of course, she was in blackface.

During Jim Crow governance in the South, schools and all public facilities were segregated. Black people were barred from serving on juries and from testifying in court. They lived in abject poverty and were subjected to daily humiliations at the hands of Whites, often from the "lowest orders" of White society. Between 1882 and 1925 nearly three thousand Black men and boys and nearly one hundred Black women and girls died at the hands of lynch mobs.

Postcards with photographs of lynching victims became a burgeoning industry — so much so that the Postmaster General banned such postcards in 1908. One of the most chilling images I ever saw was on one of these post cards. It was of a little White girl, probably aged about ten, shabbily dressed, her dirty face illuminated by torch light, smiling and looking up at the feet of several dead Black men and boys hanging from a tree. I could only think — look what they've done to her soul.

Lynchings were sometimes advertised in newspapers days before they happened and people traveled miles on trains to watch and take part. People who participated in a lynching were almost never arrested and charged with a crime, and in the rare event that anyone was brought to trial, they were acquitted in state courts by all-White juries.

The first bill to make lynching a federal crime was introduced into Congress in 1922. Northern Democrats joined forces with Southern Democrats to defeat bill after bill because Northern Democrats needed Southern Democrats' votes to pass their legislative agenda, such as Roosevelt's New Deal. A bill to make lynching a federal crime was not passed by Congress until 2022. It was sponsored by two Black Senators, Kamala Harris and Corey Booker.

Chicago, a favorite destination. Black people in the Jim Crow South had nowhere to turn. They were emphatically not welcome in the North or West. Nevertheless, a number of Black people began moving North out of desperation, often to escape a lynching, and Chicago was a favorite destination because it was the center for the only two industries in the North that would hire Black people — the meatpacking industry and the railroad industry — both offering dirty, dangerous work.

Chicago was a favorite destination as well, because of two men, George Pullman and Robert Abbott. George Pullman began to manufacture sleeping cars for railroads in a factory outside Chicago just after the Civil War. He recruited newly freed Black men to be sleeping car porters reasoning that they would work for little pay and that they would exhibit the "proper humility" in dealing with White passengers.

Because Chicago was a railroad hub, many Pullman porters made Chicago their home base. In 1959, nearly half-century after the beginning of the First Great Migration, when I took my first teaching job teaching seventh grade at Fiske Elementary School in Chicago's Black Woodlawn area, two of my students, a brother and sister, were children of a Pullman porter. That made them members of a prominent family in the community. One of these children was Minnie Riperton who was on a path to stardom as a jazz singer in the 1970s when she died of breast cancer at age 31. The actor, singer, and comedian Maya Rudolph is Minnie Riperton's daughter.

Robert Abbott was a twenty-three year old Black student at the Hampton Institute in Virginia who came to Chicago in 1893 to sing at the Chicago Columbian Exposition with the "Hampton Choir and Quartet." He made Chicago his home, and in 1905 he launched one of the nation's first Black newspapers, *The Chicago Defender*, with a run of 300 copies.

By 1915 *The Chicago Defender* had a weekly circulation of 16,000 and by 1920 its circulation reached 230,000 copies per week. Robert Abbott became one of America's first Black millionaires. He travelled frequently in Europe where he stayed in the finest hotels, except for American-owned fine hotels. American-owned fine hotels refused to rent to "Negroes!"

The Chicago Defender became one of the nation's most influential Black newspapers. It published stories that appeared nowhere else including vivid descriptions of lynchings that were committed with the connivance of white police and politicians including mayors, governors, and senators.

It was among the newspapers that published the work of Ida B. Wells who had been born a slave in 1862 and rose to become a famous journalist and anti-lynching crusader. She exposed the myth that most Black men who were lynched had raped a White woman. The "crime" was more likely to be a lack of humility — real or imagined — in an interaction with a White person. Wells was identified by the federal government in the 1920s as a dangerous subversive because of her anti-lynching reporting.

Beyond just honest reporting, *The Chicago Defender* presented Chicago as a promised land with abundant jobs available for Black workers, and as a lively city where Black people commonly went to theaters, ate at nice restaurants, attended sports events, and danced all night in the hottest nightclubs. It had a full entertainment section.

It ran advertisements for grooming products for Black men and beauty products for Black women. It ran migrant success stories and stories about prominent Black Chicagoans. It included articles and editorials that explicitly encouraged Black southern readers to move North. It even printed copies of train schedules and job listings.

Part of *the Chicago Defender's* circulation was the work of Pullman porters who smuggled bundles of *The Defender* into the South on their Illinois Central Pullman cars where each clandestine copy was passed from person to person and read aloud wherever Black people congregated. A Black person did not want to get caught with a copy of *The Chicago Defender* in the Jim Crow South.

Ironically, White Southerners often objected to Black people—the source of cheap labor—moving North. And so Black people often got a ride to a town where they would not be recognized to board a train North. If they were recognized on a railroad platform with luggage in their hometown they would surely come to grief.

Looking back, I wish I had based some of my reading and language arts lessons at Fiske Elementary School on *The Chicago Defender*. But who am I kidding? Even in 1959 a teacher would not want to get caught having students reading stories from *The Chicago Defender* in a Chicago public school classroom. At the very least, they would be accused of being a troublemaker, and more likely of being a Communist. And if they did not have tenure, which I did not at the time, they would most certainly be fired outright– "without cause."

The Great Migrations. Before and during World War I, industries in the North began to boom, and there were shortages of workers. As a result, they began to hire Black workers and Black people began to move North in great numbers. It became known as the First Great Migration, and the Southside of Chicago became a tinderbox with the continuing, often violent, rivalries among ethnic Whites (particularly white Catholics) and an all-out war on Black people culminating in the summer of 1919 Chicago riot.

The riot began on what had been a mutually agreed upon, self-segregated beach on Lake Michigan on the Southside of Chicago. A Black man, probably innocently, wandered onto the wrong side of the beach. The riot lasted seven days. Twenty-three Black people and fifteen White people died. There were more than 500 people injured — two-thirds of them Black. Over one thousand people — mostly Black — lost their homes.

In the decades leading up to World War II, war industries in the North began to boom once again which occasioned the Second Great Migration of Black people out of the South and into the North. Chicago was once again a favorite destination. By the end of World War II one and a half million Black people had moved from the South to the North and the Black population of Chicago that had been less than 2% before World War I had grown to 14% - a seven-fold increase - and the Black Belt, a narrow corridor extending

128

from 22nd Street to 31St.Street along State Street, simply could not hold the number of Black people coming north for a better life.

Covenants, Redlining, and Panic-Peddlers. Black families had been kept from moving into White neighborhoods in northern cities primarily by violence but also by laws and government policies. White neighborhoods had been legally "protected" from the flood of Black people coming to Chicago by "covenants" that restricted the ownership of property outside the Black Belt to "Whites Only."

My mother once told me that there was a covenant on our house on Union Avenue restricting ownership to Caucasian Christians—meaning "no Blacks or Jews!" These covenants were usually not enforced against Jewish families, but I did not know of any Jewish people who owned property in our neighborhood other than a family that lived above the baby carriage shop they owned at 78th and Halsted.

Covenants had a history of court challenges, but they were not overturned in Chicago until 1940 when a lawsuit was brought by Carl Hansberry, a prosperous Black Chicago businessman. He was the father of Lorraine Hansberry, who wrote *A Raisin in the Sun*, a widely acclaimed play that appeared on Broadway and was made into a movie starring Sidney Poitier. It portrayed a Black family on the Southside of Chicago in the 1950s as they considered several ways the family might spend an unexpected insurance payout. Buying a home in an all-White neighborhood was one option.

As soon as the covenants were overturned, banks adopted a new policy— "redlining." Lines were drawn on city street maps separating white and Black neighborhoods and banks would not make loans on properties on the Black side of the line. When Black people moved across these red lines, the lines were redrawn. There was nothing illegal about this. It was just "sound business practice." Banks were protecting their depositors from losses on "risky loans." And so, even though real estate covenants had been overturned by this time, custom, "sound business practices," and the threat of violence still kept Black people out of White neighborhoods and the burgeoning new suburbs.

The 1944 GI Bill of Rights enabled returning World War II veterans to get low interest, low down-payment, government-guaranteed home loans that enabled a whole generation of White families to buy homes and build equity that benefited their children and future generations. Six of my brothers and sisters and their families benefitted from GI Bill of Rights home loans.

Although the GI Bill did not discriminate against Black GIs explicitly, most Black veterans were not able to take advantage of its home-loan provisions because of a cruel "Catch 22." The government did not loan the money to the veterans directly from the United States Treasury; veterans had to get a loan from a commercial bank, and the government guaranteed the loan. But because of redlining, commercial banks would not make loans for mortgages in Black neighborhoods, and so Black people were still excluded from White neighborhoods.

As Black families began to move into neighborhoods adjacent to the Black Belt, a new profession was born. "Panic Peddlers" were real estate agents who descended upon changing neighborhoods telling White homeowners, "The first to sell gets a fair price. If you wait you will get half what your property is worth." They would buy up a house that had been valued at $15,000 for $10,000, and a week later they'd sell it for $16,000 to a Black buyer.

Of course, Black buyers couldn't get a mortgage from any bank because of redlining and flat-out race discrimination. They had to borrow "on contract" from a loan shark at exorbitant interest, and they didn't own their homes until the last payment was made. Many contract buyers lost their homes because they failed to make just one payment and they saw their homes resold to other hapless victims. This resulted in the practice of several Black families going in on a single house with the result of overcrowding and neighborhood degradation—proof to angry, frightened Whites that hatred of Black people was justified.

By 1950, home ownership on the Southside of Chicago was going from White to Black at a rate of a block a week, and the racism that had always been rife among Whites became more and more virulent. As soon as the first Black family moved into a White neighborhood, banks redlined that neighborhood, and White homeowners were facing financial ruin, and the hundreds of butcher shops, grocery stores, clothing stores, lawyers, dentists, taverns, and restaurants on streets like 79th Street and on Halsted Street that had steadfastly refused to cater to Black people were facing financial ruin as well.

Before 1850, the White population of the United States was made up almost entirely of Protestants from Great Britain and Western Europe. The Irish Potato Famine between 1845 and 1852 produced a massive wave of Irish immigration into the United States, and Irish Catholics became the nation's second largest-ethnic group.

Long before the Potato Famine, there had been a centuries-long effort by the English to subjugate the people of Ireland, and suppression of the Catholic religion in Ireland played a prominent role in that effort. It has been proposed that the English invented the concept of race and of racial superiority in their efforts to subjugate the Irish. Race became a useful concept later for excusing the British participation in the slave trade and later still for excusing their subjugating the people of the British Empire. When the Irish began to appear in the United States, "White" Protestant Americans adopted the racist anti-Catholic attitudes toward them that were already well-established by the English.

Irish immigration began in earnest just prior to the Mexican American War (1846-1848), and the United States Army recruited many of these Irish immigrants and dispatched them to the then-current southwest border. Their American-born officers treated these young Irishmen with scorn, and compelled them to attend Protestant religious services.

However, because of their shared religion, the young Irishmen felt an affinity with the Mexicans and when they attended Mass it was in Mexican churches with Mexican priests and Mexican congregations. Somewhere between one hundred and several hundred United States soldiers switched sides and fought on the side of Mexico in what became known as the Saint Patrick's Battalion. After the United States won the war, 50 Saint Patrick's Battalion members were executed by the U.S. Army — the largest mass execution by the Army in United States history.

By the 1850s the "Know-Nothings," a secret society of Protestant men, was formed to limit the immigration and naturalization of Catholics, whom they saw as un-American and whose allegiance was to the Pope in Rome. At its height, the Know-Nothings included more than one hundred members of Congress and eight governors.

In the 1880s, there was a second wave of Catholic immigrants into the United States, this time, from southern and eastern Europe. These were the "Dark Europeans" — Greeks, Italians, Hungarians, Bohemians (that is, Czechs), Poles, and other speakers of Slavic languages. In addition, there were as many as four million Jewish immigrants. Once again, these newcomers, along with the Irish and Mexicans were not considered "White" by White Protestant Americans.

By 1920, the population of the Southside of Chicago was a collection of second- and third-generation Irish, Italian, Greek, Hungarian, Polish, and Bohemian neighborhoods with a sprinkling of Jewish families throughout. These communities were always on the brink of war with one another and agreed only on their hatred of Black people, who made up only two percent of Chicago's population and were confined to the "Black Belt."

Terms of abuse abounded: Mick, Bohunk, Spic, Whop, Pollock, Kraut, Grease Ball, Dago, Kike, and, of course, Coon, and N*gger. The Irish, Dark Europeans, and Mexicans were predominantly Catholic, but the Church made little effort to address ethnic intolerance, let alone racial intolerance. In fact, the Catholic Church's establishment of ethnic parishes (Irish, Polish, and so on) only exacerbated the hostility between these groups.

In the one square mile neighborhood known as "The Back of the Yards" there were eleven Catholic churches — two Polish, one Lithuanian, one Italian, two German, one Slovak, one Croatian, two Irish, and one Bohemian. Some of these parishes had schools taught by orders of nuns associated with ethnic identities.

Each parish was led by priests with corresponding ethnicity who expressed nothing but scorn for priests from rival parishes. They often did not speak to one another when they passed on the street. One newspaper reported that the Lithuanians saw Poles as enemies. The Slovaks were anti-Bohemian, and the Germans were suspected by all four nationalities. Jewish people were generally abominated, and the Irish called everyone else "foreigners."

134

Eugenics. The idea that ethnic groups could be ranked in terms of superiority was a widely held view, and it had a certain amount of support from, of all places, the scientific community. Darwin published *The Origin of the Species* in 1859. Within twenty-five years the idea of genetically inherited traits had become widely understood, and Francis Galton, a British anthropologist, proposed that the human race could be improved by selective breeding of people with a superior genetic makeup.

This proposition became known as *Eugenics* and it was widely accepted by highly respectable institutions, such as the Carnegie and Rockefeller Foundations, the Women's Christian Temperance Union, and the National League of Women Voters. Many highly respected American universities offered courses in Eugenics.

Eugenics quickly morphed into the idea that certain ethnic groups had superior genes and should be encouraged to procreate while other ethnic groups had inferior genes and should be discouraged from procreating. Not surprisingly, White Anglo-Saxon Western European Protestants who were politically, economically, and socially dominant came to be seen as genetically superior, while less powerful ethnic groups came to be seen as genetically suspect.

Despite the circularity of this reasoning, Eugenics became highly respectable. Eugenicists were asked to testify before congressional committees considering immigration policy as late as 1924, and as late as the 1930s, the unofficial position of the Catholic Church was that interracial and interethnic marriages should be discouraged because they produced offspring with the worst traits of each parent.

The Eugenics movement disappeared in the 1930s and 1940s with the rise of Hitler, his "Master Race" ravings, and the horrifying Holocaust that followed; however, "Master Race" thinking has hardly disappeared. The difference is that today such ideas are not considered respectable, certainly not by the scientific and educated community.

Chapter 13.

CATHOLIC PARISHES and WHITE FLIGHT

I was barely conscious of racial strife while I was in grammar school. In our neighborhood Black and White people passed each other on the streets without incident and we were comfortable sitting together in the same seat on a streetcar. But Black people would not be waited on at a store or restaurant in a White neighborhood. Black people came into our neighborhood only to work as cleaning women or as "coal men."

Most homes then were heated with coal furnaces. Coal deliveries were dumped onto the street close to the curb in front of your house, and a Black man — always a Black man — shoveled the coal into a wheelbarrow, wheeled it down your gangway to a basement window, and dumped it into your coal bin, one wheelbarrow-full after the other. It was dirty, backbreaking work that no White men wanted. Children in my neighborhood were not expected to speak to these workers.

When I was in seventh grade there was a "march" of White students protesting the fact that Black students would attend Parker High School the next September. Parker was the public high school for the district just north of the Calumet district. This was the first time I ever heard the word *march* used to mean a politically motivated street demonstration.

The march did not stop Black students from attending Parker, and when I started to attend Calumet in 1949 there was already a sprinkling of Black students attending. There were never any racial incidents at Calumet that I knew of, but I do not believe I ever spoke to a Black student. By 1953, my graduating class was about ten percent Black.

And while I never spoke to a Black student at Calumet, having daily contact with Black students tended to make me more tolerant and less afraid of black people than most of the people around me. But my *not going to St. Leo High School* had a more profound effect on my attitude toward race than anything I experienced at Calumet.

A study in the 1960s found that Catholic high school boys were considerably more bigoted than public school boys. That was certainly true of the Catholic high school boys I knew in the 1950s. And it was not just racial hatred that animated my friends who attended Catholic high schools. It was anti-Semitism as well. At St. Leo High School they read *The Merchant of Venice*, and Shylock was presented as a "dirty Jew" and Shakespeare was presented approvingly as a rabid anti-Semite. It is noteworthy that of all of Shakespeare's plays, they chose that one. At Calumet we did not read *The Merchant of Venice*. We read *Julius Caesar* and *Macbeth*.

Of course, at Calumet there were Jewish teachers and students and there were Black students as well, and so there was never any blatant anti-Semitism or racism, at least in the classroom. Sitting in classrooms with Black students and knowing many of them were getting better grades than I—admittedly a low bar—made me less prejudiced toward Black people and less afraid of them than my Catholic high school friends were.

I first heard that "Jews killed Jesus" from a student at Quigley, the Chicago Archdiocese high school for boys preparing for the priesthood. Another Quigley boy told me, "Jesus taught that we should love our neighbors—but not n*ggers!" The oldest boy in a prominent St. Leo parish family (the father owned a tavern on 79th Street) became a priest. He went to seminary in Milwaukee because a newly minted priests in the Chicago archdiocese seminary might be sent to a Black parish. None of this was considered shameful. It's just the way it was.

In 1955, several of my friends who graduated from St. Leo High School went on to DePaul University in Chicago, the nation's largest Catholic institution of higher education at that time. DePaul had recently accepted a few Black students for the first time in its history, and three Black freshmen had the temerity to pledge my friend's fraternity. The fraternity met "intensively"—as frat boys would have said, self-importantly in those days, and after hours of discussion, the fraternity chaplain suggested that they take one boy—the one with the worst academic record. He would be more likely than the others to flunk out in his first semester.

My friend was full of admiration for the chaplain's *realpolitik* savvy. I wonder if the priest/professor didn't have some idea of how he might influence the student's academic success. That might be too conspiratorial, but it's not inconsistent with the way the boys I knew who went to Catholic schools at the time talked. I didn't ever encourage this kind of talk from my Catholic high school friends, but I didn't discourage it either—well-aware that my silence was seen as acquiescence.

Mr. Tarr died in 1953, and Mrs. Tarr asked me to sit in the butcher shop one afternoon with a real estate salesman who was showing the shop to prospective buyers. No doubt owing to the fact that 78th and Halsted Street was "threatened" by this date, there were no prospective buyers. That left the salesman and me to make conversation.

Our conversation soon turned to race relations—a topic it was assumed two White people would agree on. He said he wondered why no one had poisoned the water supply to the Black Belt, and I said I thought there was probably only one water supply for the whole Southside, and so that was not feasible. I should have been shocked, but I wasn't. I did not think this was a serious proposal. It was just the way people talked.

It was around this time that I came to understand that sophistication is not simply knowing the right things, but it is also having the right beliefs and reflecting them in what you said and how you said it. I began to say "negro" rather than "n*gger" and of course I would be called a "n*gger lover." Sticks and stones!

Years later I was one of only four White faculty members in a faculty of thirty-five at Fiske Elementary School when I taught there in 1959, my first year of teaching, and I was the only White faculty member who ate my brown bag lunch with a dozen or so of my Black fellow teachers in the cramped supplies storeroom on the third floor of the building that passed for a "teacher's lounge."

I occasionally drove a Black teacher home after school when her car was in the shop. I attended the Chicago Teachers Union Annual St. Patrick's Day corned beef and green beer stag party with a Black male colleague. I drove, and I picked him up and dropped him off at home. And so, I established some cred with my Black colleagues at Fiske without thinking about it much.

One day during lunch the conversation turned to the fact my colleagues were planning to join a picket line in front of a movie theater near the school on a busy street that separated the Black and White neighborhoods. The theater did not sell tickets to Black people. I became aware that this conversation was being aimed at me.

No one said, "Pat, would you join us? A White face in our picket line would make a real difference," but the message was pretty clear. I simply did not tumble, and the incident was over. I don't think my Black colleagues thought any less of me, but they had hoped for more.

This was one of those "Road Not Taken" occasions. I would have crossed a line and committed an overt act in support for integration, and I wasn't ready to do that. I wasn't afraid that any physical harm would come to me, but these demonstrations sometimes appeared on local newscasts, and I was afraid that my family, particularly Brud and Jim, would find out. I was not prepared to become ostracized from the Finn Family. I never have wanted to do that really.

My parents accepted the racial status quo of Chicago during my grammar school years. Although Black people were always referred to as n*ggers in my home, I never had the impression that they hated Black people. My mother once commented that she always said hello to the Black cleaning lady from the boarding house on our block. She would, of course; she had a kind heart.

But the fact that she commented on it reflected the fact that most people would not have politely acknowledged a Black woman's presence on our block no matter how obvious it was that she had a "legitimate" reason to be there. My mother also once told me that at some point my father had thyroid surgery at Cook County Hospital during the Depression, and a Black man in the next bed helped to get a nurse when my father was in difficulty and he may have saved my father's life. And so, motivated by the financial ruin she faced if the value of our house cratered when Black people moved into St. Leo Parish, my mother did not hate Black people.

I'm from St. Leo. While the entire White population of the Southside of Chicago felt threatened, Catholics arguably had more reason to feel threatened than others. Unlike Protestants and Jews who lived scattered throughout the city, often miles from the church or synagogue they attended, Catholics lived within parish boundaries, and they felt a strong sense of identity, not just with their church, but also with the geographical location that comprised their parish.

Newspaper advertisements often listed available apartments and homes by parish – "Holy Redeemer 2 Flat" or "St. Sabina Bungalow." Catholics responded to the question "Where are you from?" with a parish name — "I'm from St. Leo" or "I'm from St. Rita." In the 1970s I was interviewed for a teaching job at the University of Illinois in Champaign by Dolores Durkin, a distinguished professor of education. She too was Catholic and from Chicago's Southside. What parish each of us was from came up in the conversation.

And finally, Chicago Catholics were overwhelmingly working-class. All of this gave rise to intense feelings of solidarity. They were indeed a society of intimates. And there were enormous financial considerations at stake. Many Catholics were descendants of immigrant groups who prospered and valued home ownership highly, and so they were more likely than non-Catholics to be homeowners. In addition, Catholic parishes owned millions of dollars in property.

St. Leo parish had an enormous church, an elementary school, a boys' high school, a residence for the Christian Brothers who taught at St. Leo High School, a convent, a rectory, a small community center with a four-lane bowling alley, and a football stadium that seated nearly a thousand. St. Sabina, the parish just west of St. Leo, had an elementary school, convent, rectory, and a community center with a full basketball court that served as a roller-skating rink after school on Friday afternoons (skate rentals in-house) and teen-age dances on Sunday evenings. I often went roller-skating there and to Sunday night dances.

And so, Catholic parishes were "immovable." But as Black families crossed parish lines, White parishioners fled nevertheless. Receipts from Sunday collections plummeted, and parishes could not cover the costs of maintaining real estate worth millions of dollars. Catholics began to fear the Chicago dioceses might go bankrupt, and if they were looking for spiritual and moral guidance from the altar on Sunday morning, they were sadly mistaken.

In 1946 Cardinal Stritch, head of the Chicago Dioceses, made a commitment to the Chicago Commission on Human Relations that all Catholic parishes and schools in the city would welcome all races and minorities. The cardinal was probably saying what he was expected to say without believing that his pledge was politically possible.

By 1950 parish priests at St. Leo began to say things like, "The right to protect our homes is as sacred as the right to defend our lives," and Chicago Catholic high schools remained all White well into the 1960s which was long after many of them were entirely surrounded by Black neighborhoods, and "the right to defend our homes" was understood to mean "by whatever means necessary."

Chapter 14.

FATHER TOLTON and JOHN LAFARGE

There were collections taken up at St. Leo Grammar School for the "Foreign Missions" in Africa and Asia, and so I assumed there were Black Catholics in Africa but not in America—certainly not in Chicago. I was wrong on both counts. In 1790 Jean Baptiste Du Sable became the first person who was not of Native American descent to settle on the land that was to become Chicago. Du Sable was born in Haiti and was both Black and Catholic, and there have been Black Catholics in Chicago ever since.

In Maryland, which was founded by the Catholic Lord Baltimore, in 1634, Jesuits baptized both slaves and free Black people and instructed them in the Catholic faith. Black converts were always taught separately from White converts, and Black congregants attended separate Masses or sat at the back of the church and received Communion after the white congregants. This custom continued throughout the South as slave states were added to the union. And so, when the Civil War ended there were already thousands of Black Catholics in the South, many of whom came north even before the two Great Migrations.

The Knights of Columbus, a Catholic fraternal organization, was founded in 1881. One of its missions was to integrate Black and White Catholic churches. Later, in 1909, the Knights of Columbus founded the Knights of Peter Claver, a Catholic fraternal organization for Black men in the South because even forty years after the abolition of slavery, integrated organizations in the South were still a dangerous proposition. I always thought the Knights of Columbus was a Catholic fraternity similar to the Masons, and so when I learned its true history, it made perfect sense that there was not a chapter at St. Leo Parish.

America's first Black Catholic priest, Father Augustus Tolton, was born into slavery in Missouri in 1854. He was baptized by his Catholic slave owner and while still an infant, he escaped with his mother to Quincy, Illinois where he was tutored by local Catholics — outside of school of course because no school in Quincy, public or Catholic, would accept a Black student. When he decided he wanted to become a priest, no Catholic Seminary in America would accept a Black student. He was accepted at last to a seminary in Rome and was ordained there in 1886. Tolton returned to his home in Quincy becoming America's first Black Catholic priest.

In 1891 he came to Chicago to establish a parish for the several hundred Black Catholics who attended Mass in the basement of an all-White Catholic church in the Black Belt.

147

Father Tolton tried to establish a Catholic school for Black children. His efforts were underwritten by Sister Katharine Drexel, who founded the Sisters of the Blessed Sacrament, a religious order of nuns dedicated to the education of "American Indian and Colored people". Sister Drexel was the millionaire heiress of George Drexel, founder of the Drexel Banking Company, which is J. P. Morgan today.

Although she could have easily financed a building for a school, she believed the Chicago Catholic Dioceses should shoulder that expense. The dispute was never resolved, and a Catholic school for Black children never came to pass. At one point the Sisters of Providence, the same order that taught at St. Leo Grammar School while I was there, considered teaching at Father Tolton's proposed school. They too abandoned the project. Father Tolton's efforts to establish a "Negro parish" with a school for Black Catholic children ended when he died of apparent exhaustion in 1897. A few hundred Black Catholics continued to attend Mass in the basement of a White Catholic Church.

By the time I was in high school, Black Catholics in Chicago numbered in the thousands and Chicago was the home of more Black Catholics than any other city in the country. They attended mass in the basements of Catholic churches on the fringe of the Black belt, and when they attended Mass in White Catholic Churches, they sat at the back and received Communion after the White congregants.

Where would we have learned this history of Black Catholics in America and in Chicago during these challenging times? Certainly not from the altar at St. Leo church. Certainly not from the brothers at St. Leo High School. Not even from the nuns at St. Leo Grammar School, despite the fact that their order was briefly involved in Father Tolton's effort to found a Catholic school for Catholic Black children in Chicago's Black Belt.

The history of Black Catholics in America and in Chicago never became part of the conversation among Chicago's White Catholics. It was one of those inconvenient truths that can be left unstated, and therefore less likely to be confronted in a society of intimates. It would have exposed the contradictions and invited challenges.

The gossip that spread excitedly and approvingly among St. Leo parishioners concerned the violence visited upon Black people by White Catholics who were motivated by the belief that the Black people were attempting to integrate a White neighborhood. In 1951, the summer after my sophomore year in high school, an apartment building owner in Cicero, a suburb west of Chicago separated from the city by a single street, Cicero Avenue, rented an apartment to a Black family.

Cicero was a heavily Bohemian and Slavic working-class suburb where sixty percent of the population was Catholic. There ensued "the Cicero Riot," wherein a mob of 4,000 Whites converged on the apartment building and threw rocks and firebombs. The rioting went on for days. Observers

149

described the mob as largely Catholic, with boys wearing letters from Catholic high schools on their sweaters. A man in the crowd was heard to remark; "I don't want those jigs sitting in the same pew with me."

Visitation, the parish located on Garfield Boulevard three miles directly north of St. Leo, was known as a "little diocese" because of the close connections between its priests and local politicians. In the late 1940s Visitation parishioners organized the Boulevard Improvement Association dedicated unapologetically to "keep Negroes out." Meetings were sometimes held in the parish hall.

When, in 1950, it was falsely rumored that one of the few Jewish homeowners living within Visitation parish boundaries had sold to a Black family, a mob gathered in front of their house chanting "dirty kikes," "Communists," and "burn the house down." Groups of men stopped unfamiliar pedestrians and accused them of being "Jews, University of Chicago students, or Communists". Among Boulevard Improvement Association members, Jews, University of Chicago students, and Communists were one and the same.

Since the 1920s the University of Chicago was believed by many Southside Catholics to be a hot bed of Communists and Jews who used integration as a way to divide Americans. While I was a student at Calumet there was a yearly essay competition for seniors; the prize was a scholarship to the University of Chicago. That scholarship went unclaimed some of those years because of the University's reputation as a hotbed of Communists.

In 1953, the year I graduated from Calumet, a home in Trumbull Park—an all-White federally supported low-cost housing project on Chicago's far Southside—was sold to a Black family. Riots ensued, and members of the Trumbull Park Neighborhood Improvement Association attacked city officials for tolerating a "carefully planned Communistic plot." By that time the nation was well into the McCarthy Era.

As they faced social and economic realities resulting from the movement of Black people into White neighborhoods, parishioners were offered no moral or spiritual guidance. Instead, on a designated Sunday every year the congregation was instructed to stand and recite an eighty-eight-word pledge to The Legion of Decency beginning with the words, "*I condemn all indecent and immoral motion pictures....*" And concluding "*...I promise to stay altogether away from places of amusement which show them as a matter of policy.*"

James T. Farrell, author of *Studs Lonigan*, observed a generation before me, "The Catholic clergy had shrunk morality to a series of do's and do not's, mainly regarding sex." Things had not gotten any better a generation later— only perhaps worse.

Beginning when I was in high school, I remained seated during the Legion of Decency Pledge. And since I did not think I was making my position clear enough, I began to leave the church during the pledge and return afterwards. I didn't want to miss Mass. My mother had no reason to know this. She would, no doubt, have seen it as more of the smart-ass bull-crap she had come to expect from me.

John LaFarge was a Jesuit teacher and writer in the 1920s and 1930s. He counted among his friends and colleagues William and Henry James, and Theodore Roosevelt. He considered racism a sin and spoke out about the conditions under which Black people were forced to live in America. His writing appeared regularly in Catholic magazines such as *America* and *Commonweal.*

In 1937 LaFarge published a book, *Interracial Justice: A Study of the Catholic Doctrine of Race Relations*, which attracted the attention of Pope Pius XI who was grappling with how to respond to Hitler's "Master Race" ravings. He asked LaFarge and two German Jesuits to write an encyclical on Catholic teaching concerning race. A published papal encyclical was considered infallible doctrine by the Catholic Church. The encyclical entitled *On the Unity of the Human Race* was delivered to Pius XI late in 1938, but it was not published because Pius XI died in 1939 and his successor Pius XII buried the encyclical, an act that was not out of character for him.

In 1999 a book was published about Pius XII entitled *Hitler's Pope.* Many critics of the book agree that that title is a little overblown, but there is plenty of evidence that when faced with choosing between a difficult moral choice and a politically expedient one, Pius XII often chose the latter. He cooperated with Mussolini and the Fascists in return for the protections and favors that Mussolini showered on the Catholic Church as he gained power in Italy.

In fact, beginning with the 1918 Communist Revolution in Russia, Leftists faced off against Fascists in many Catholic countries, such as Italy, Spain, and Mexico, and the Catholic Church always sided with the Fascists. That is understandable, of course, because the Communists were atheists and they committed many atrocities against both priests and nuns in Spain and Mexico.

The Catholic Church liturgy did present certain challenges to the virulent racism that gripped Catholic parishes as the movement of Black families threatened the economic well-being of parishioners, parishes, and the entire dioceses. On the thirtieth Sunday of every year Matthew's gospel is read aloud containing the lines:

> You shall love the Lord your God with all your heart, and with all your soul, and with all your mind. This is the great and first commandment. And a second is like it. You shall love your neighbor as yourself. On these two commandments depend all the law and the prophets.

This of course begs the question, "Who is my neighbor?" — The Jewish merchants and professional people on Halsted Street? My Protestant neighbors? The Polish Catholics who go to Sacred Heart? The Bohemian Catholics who go to Saints Cyril and Methodius? The Italian Catholics who go St. Mary

153

of Padua? The Black Catholics who attend Mass in the basement of St. Elizabeth Church in Chicago's Black Belt? Or indeed, all the Black people fleeing the Jim Crow South and bursting out of the Black Belt that could no longer hold them? And so, when "Matthew" was read from the altar at St. Leo Church, I am sure it was read without comment, and greeted with stony silence from "the faithful."

Chapter 15.

WHITE FLIGHT

In 1950, near the end of my freshman high school year, Monsignor Shewbridge, the pastor of St. Leo Parish since 1918, died. I remember him as a tall, stately, dignified man whom I saw occasionally on Emerald Avenue when he walked from the rectory to the church or to his car. He sometimes visited St. Leo Grammar School on report card day and distributed report cards in two or three classrooms. In the upper grades, after the report cards were distributed, he would make a fuss over a few outstanding scholars, encourage us all to continue our hard work, and tell Sister what a fine job she was doing. Sister would smile and bow her head slightly to acknowledge the compliment.

While he was talking, Monsignor would put his hand on the shoulder of one of the boys seated at a front desk and begin squeezing the boy's shoulder between his thumb and fingers. All the while he would continue to talk, taking no notice of the boy as he began to squirm with pain. We all knew what the game was. The boy would eventually utter a cry and Monsignor would release his grip and smile down at the boy, and say, "Good man!" Monsignor Shewbridge was a nice man. I liked him.

Right Reverend Monsignor Patrick Molloy. The Chicago Catholic Dioceses sent Father Patrick Molloy to replace Monsignor Shewbridge. Father Molloy was not tall, stately, dignified, or saintly. He was a man of average height with a potbelly and the red nose of an alcoholic—which he undoubtedly was. He was not a nice man. He was a despicable, contemptible man. As a young priest in the 1920s, Molloy had been a go-between for two famous Prohibition-Era Chicago mobsters—Al Capone and Bugsy Moran.

When $600,000 disappeared between the two gangs, Cardinal Mundelein, the head of the Chicago Catholic Archdioceses, was warned in a telephone call "If Molloy isn't out of town by midnight, he'll be at the bottom of the Chicago River by morning." Within the next few hours Father Molloy was on his way to Argentina where he remained until the end of the Prohibition Era.

Molloy was an unabashed racist. He spoke disparagingly about "Pollocks, "Dagos," and "N*ggers" in public settings—including from the altar during Mass on Sunday morning. He said to a Black Catholic seminarian, "The church has been doing fine without people like you, and it would continue to do so." When a Black woman appeared at the rectory to register as a parishioner, Molloy told her there was no room for "you people," and he added, "I don't give a damn about him"—referring to the Cardinal who was at least offering lip-service to the integration of Catholic parishes. When the first Black Catholics began to attend Sunday Mass at St. Leo, Molloy occasionally asked "the burr-heads" to leave the church during the Mass.

Molloy bought up all the property adjacent to parish property (including our house). He had all the houses torn down and he converted the empty parcels into a parking lot to ensure that no Black families would live adjacent to the church. He paid my mother what the property had been valued at before the area was threatened by the changing demography of the Southside of Chicago.

While Father Molloy was pastor of St. Leo, the dioceses bestowed upon him the title *Right Reverend Monsignor*, and Cardinal Stritch, Mayor Richard J. Daley, other politicians, policemen, parishioners, and a few old-time members of the mob, attended the celebration party.

I learned at St. Leo Grammar School that the 4th century Council of Nicaea proclaimed that the Catholic Church is One, Holy, Catholic, and Apostolic: It is "one" in the sense that it is the same everywhere for everyone; it is "holy" in that it is spiritual and inspires spirituality; it is "apostolic" in that it traces its history back to the apostles, and it is "catholic" in the sense that it is universal.

That is the stuff that Catholic-school education is made of, and I found it interesting in the way I found the mood and aspect of verbs interesting. I have never had any occasion to question whether the Catholic church was Catholic or Apostolic. But I began to question whether the church was One when it was faced with the prospect of Black people – Black Catholics in particular – crossing parish boundaries in Chicago during my adolescence.

Black Catholics had been attending Mass in the basement of a White Catholic Church near the Black Belt, and the Cardinal advised White Catholics to stop attending services with the Black Catholics because it would embarrass them – that is, it would embarrass the Black Catholics. One apologist for segregation of Catholic schools claimed, "Negro Children have the right to a Catholic education, but they do not have the right to get it seated next to White children." Flat out racism is bad enough. Racism wrapped in sanctimonious twaddle is insufferable.

By the time I started high school I began to seriously question whether the Catholic Church was Holy. In those days churches were commonly left open during the day so people could "make a visit." Since I lived so close to St. Leo church, I walked past it often, and as a boy of eight or ten I would very occasionally make a visit.

I never intended for anyone to know about this, and no one ever did. Being alone, or nearly alone (there were sometimes one or two other "visitors") in that vast structure with its altar, and golden tabernacle, and thirty-foot pillars holding up the inspiringly painted ceiling, and statues, and paintings, and sometimes with the smell of incense, or burning bee's wax candles—it was awe inspiring. I felt I was in a holy place, and I did feel a little holy.

But living just a half block from the church and rectory, I frequently saw priests on the street, and I never associated them with holiness, except perhaps Monsignor Shewbridge. And when the Cardinal sent Father Molloy to replace Monsignor Shewbridge, and Molloy was seemingly accepted by the priests of the parish, I had no further allusions about priests being holy. And from what I heard from my Catholic high school friends, the priests and brothers who taught them were not holy, and they were not interested in inspiring holiness in their students.

I did not feel holy at Mass. Going to Mass on Sunday was an obligation. You did it or you would go to Hell. It was mostly in Latin and as a little boy I could not even see what was going on at the altar. By the time I could see what was happening on the altar, it all seemed mechanical, certainly not inspiring. I stood, sat, and kneeled when the rest of the congregation did, and I waited for the Mass to be over.

When the priest read from the gospel, Mass was about halfway over, and I just hoped the sermon would be short. I never once found a sermon memorable or inspiring. The bells announcing the "consecration" were a welcome signal that Mass would be over soon. And when the priest faced the congregation and said, *"I'te missa est,"* and the altar boys responded, *"Deo gratias,"* it was over—at last.

In the 1960's when they first began to say the Mass in English that exchange, (*"I'te missa est."* *"Deo gratias."*) was translated literally. The priest said, "Go! The Mass has ended." To which the altar boys responded, "Thanks be to God." The irony was — I just can't find the word. Today you will hear at the end of the Mass something that does not provoke mirth, such as "Go in peace!" followed by a joyous hymn.

The nuns at St. Leo Grammar School did seem to value holiness and they sometimes inspired a feeling of holiness in me, such as on the rare occasion I saw them in ranks, two by two, heads bowed, walking down Emerald Avenue to 7:15 a.m. Mass which they attended every weekday morning.

But when I started high school and started working at Tarr's there was no time for making "visits," and I was no longer with one of those lovely women for several hours most days of my life. And then there was the Right Reverend Monsignor Patrick Molloy. I've looked up antonyms for *holy*. *Irreligious* and *corrupt* are top hits. In describing the Right Reverend Monsignor Patrick Molloy, I would add *ignorant, disgusting,* and *contemptible*.

Smart-ass teen. I sympathized with my mother and everyone else around me regarding the stark fact that property values did plummet when Black people moved across the last "red line" and into your neighborhood, and I understood that our house on Union Avenue was the sum total of my mother's capital, but I insisted upon talking about it with the explicit, middle-class, society of strangers' way of expressing myself that I had learned at Calumet High School.

Was Father Molloy's hateful rhetoric and behavior what we ought to expect from the altar during Sunday Mass? Wasn't his elevation to "Right Reverend Monsignor" horrifying, considering his sordid past and loathsome, alcohol-fueled behavior? Was it reprehensible that he was feted by the Cardinal, the mayor of Chicago, aldermen and Prohibition era mobsters at the celebration party on that occasion?

During high school years my life was going to school (or not), going to work at Tarr's (always), going home, and because I got home after my mother, Jack, and Mickey had eaten, I would find stuff on the kitchen counter for me to prepare my own dinner. Two uncooked pork chops or hamburger patties and a can of green beans was typical fare. Then I'd watch one of the sparse offerings on TV (there were only three channels) or walk down the alley to Murphy's. I was busy, and so I was not bored or lonely. I was not unhappy.

By this time life at our house on Union Avenue had changed dramatically. My father had died, and my older brothers and sisters had married and left Union Avenue. My mother was no longer washing, ironing, and cooking for eleven people, and there were no longer those Monday washdays in the basement or Tuesday ironing days. By this time, we had an automatic gas hot water heater in the

161

basement and an automatic washer and gas dryer in the former "butler's pantry" off the kitchen, and many laundry items that once needed ironing were now wash and wear.

At the same time, I could arrange my schedule so that I was home from school by two or two-thirty every day, and since Tarr did not expect me at work until around three-thirty, I was home for an hour or more every afternoon, and on the many days I skipped school I was home all day before going to work, and when I got home from work at Tarr's, it was often just my mother and me watching television. And so we spent a lot of time together, just the two of us. She was in fact my best friend.

We got along well, and we really liked being together. One of my fondest memories is of one night when the two of us were watching a sitcom on television. Two characters in the show, a young man and middle-aged woman, were talking about the woman's son and how ungrateful he was.

The young man who was played by an actor known for his nerdy, Jewish shtick says, "Wasn't it Shakespeare who said, 'How sharper than a serpent's tooth it is to have a thankless child!'" The conversation continues and the woman quotes this line, or more accurately, misquotes this line repeatedly: "A thankless child is like a toothless serpent." "A toothless child is like a thankless serpent." It was very funny and both my mother and I laughed. Years later one of us could allude to a "toothless child," and the other would get the joke.

But as time went on, we spent less and less time laughing together. My mother would come home from an afternoon Altar and Rosary meeting and find me there, and she would want to share what she had learned from Father So-and-so who had been a missionary in Mexico and who had told the women at the meeting that there is no rape in Mexico.

The implication was that there was no rape in Mexico because Mexico is a devoutly Catholic country, and I, not buying it, said, "That's because they have fourteen-year-old prostitutes in Mexico." There was a flash of anger in my mother's eyes, but the conversation ended there. How I wish today that I had not been such a smart-ass then or on numerous other occasions like it. *How sharper than a serpent's tooth it is to have a thankless child.*

Part of it was simply that I was becoming a smart-ass teen-ager, which is something I would have grown out of. But soon our points of contention were far more immediate than the question of prostitution in Mexico. Since the end of World War II, Black people were fleeing from the Jim Crow South to cities in the North, and they were bursting out of the Black ghettoes where they had always been confined. This created the greatest social, political, economic, and moral crisis of my lifetime.

My response to the crisis was pretty much the racist response of everyone around me. What my mother and I did begin to disagree about was the response of the Catholic Church to the crisis — particularly the conflict between church doctrine and what was happening all around me. I wanted to

163

discuss it—to argue about it as we might have in a Calumet classroom, in a society of strangers. This was alienating me from the Catholic, working-class, society of intimates that I had been born into—and, sadly, it was alienating me from my mother most of all.

Chapter 16.

CODA

I bring my memoir to a close with my high school years. I would have loved to go on. I have always enjoyed writing, but I am approaching 90 and it's time to wrap it up.

After high school I realized a job in the building trades would not be possible for me due to Erb's palsy, and white-collar work without a college degree would mean a life of very low pay. There was a desperate need for teachers, and so I enrolled at Chicago Teachers College (which is now Chicago State University), and that began my academic career. After four years I got a degree and worked as a teacher in Chicago's Black Belt, and at Fort Greely, an army post in Alaska, and at Ridgewood high school in a suburb of Chicago, and once again on the Southside of Chicago.

It was at Ridgewood high school that I met my wife, Mary. She and I have two daughters, Molly and Amy, and four "grands". Molly's are Harry and PJ; Amy's are Lewis and Moe.

Meanwhile I earned a master's degree, again at Chicago Teachers College, and finally, I attended the University of Chicago where I earned a Ph.D. While at the University of Chicago I was granted a Fellowship that allowed me to travel to Edinburgh, Scotland to finish my dissertation. I returned to the United States, taught for one year at Rutgers University, filling in for a professor on sabbatical leave, and then I accepted a position at The State University of New York at Buffalo where I taught for 30 years.

It was during those 30 years I wrote two textbooks for students studying to become teachers, one on teaching reading and one on teaching writing. The year I retired I published *Literacy with an Attitude* which became one of its publisher's (The State University of New York Press) best sellers of all times.

And so, goodbye to all that. I look forward to continuing a long and happy retirement.

Made in the USA
Las Vegas, NV
08 November 2024

11385987R00101